EASTERN EUROPEAN ARCHEOLOGY

TOMOR: THE FATHER OF PAGAN GODS

by

Besim Dervishi

HELIOS
PUBLISHING

© 2022 Besim Dervishi

ISBN: 978-1-7371175-3-7

Eastern European Archeology   Tomor: The
Mountain of Gods

HELIOS PUBLISHING

heliospublishing.us

Copyrights© 2022 by Besim Dervishi All rights reserved. No parts of this publication should be reproduced, distributed by any means including photocopying, recording, or any other electronic or manual methods without the prior permission of the publisher, except for brief quotations embodied in reviews and non-commercial uses permitted by copyright law.

TABLE OF CONTENTS

INTRODUCTION 5

BETWEEN THE LEGEND AND THE TRUTH: FROM PAGANISM TO CHRISTIANITY TO OUR DAYS..36

THE CIRCULAR STRUCTURE OF STONES AT THE NORTHERN TOP OF TOMOR 75

DODONA CITY 90

ANNOTATED BIBLIOGRAPHY 110

"...Even after Albanian independence had been secured, patriots remained convinced that the only solution to the divisive dichotomy between Islam and Christianity was their substitution for Albanians. Thus Andon Chako, using the pen name Chajupi in his book "Memedheu" (Motherland), included a poem about Mount Tomor. On its peak stood a shrine where ancient Albanians resorted to consulting the oracle about their fate..."

Edwin E. Jacques [1]

---

[1] "The Albanians: An Ethnic History from Prehistoric Times to the Present", page 398

INTRODUCTION

Every person, state, or nation should know their history. Nations must know the way their ancestors lived and prospered. I believe that historical and archeological studies must serve as a foundation for the unification of nation-states and not their separation. When used for political and expansionist purposes, history and archeology have resulted in dramatic consequences for the humanity. Eastern and Southern Europe have often been a battleground to fulfill chauvinist and territorial claims by various political actors in the region, and for that matter, Albania became one of the first countries occupied by Italy on the verge of WWII, on April 7, 1939. Hence, before the invasion, it is worth mentioning that the Italian Regime while Mussolini was in power promoted various archeological expeditions in Albania and Egypt from 1920-1930. Through expeditions in Butrint, in the south of Albania, the Italian researchers sought to shed light on archeological evidence that would justify the fascist invasion of Albania and other Balkan nations. Nazis in Germany in the 1930s and 1940s followed the same method by sending their historical and archeological expeditions to China and India. Hence, archeology and history have been used as "red meat for nationalists" since the mid-1800s, the era known as the "nation" building in Europe.

The exploitation of history and archeology for nationalist purposes during these critical years led to major conflicts and wars. Two wars took place in the Illyrian Peninsula (Balkans), not to mention WWI and WWII.

Inherently, archeology and history are often used to justify internal or international conflicts on territorial claims. Such conflicts have caused devastations, ethnic cleansing, and other misfortunes for small nations or ethnicities.

The opposite happens when these fields of study: Archeology, history, and language or studies and transcripts of ancient writing, are explored by researchers who are passionate about scientific evidence. These scholars stay away from territorial claims and do not misuse epistemology for a political agenda. For these researchers, discovering new historical and archaeological facts, ancient artifacts, and writings on stones is evidence that helps the public understand the truth about civilizations. When there are scientific debates among researchers, bringing new archaeological and historical facts in their books and works enhances theoretical evidence. It sheds light on many events that go beyond assumptions. For that matter, I strongly suggest that archeological findings, ancient writings, and historical documents be published without manipulation or hidden agendas. When recorded, archaeological and linguistic facts are presented without distortion, without manipulation, but objectively, they help the public to see the truth in the eye.

In this book, I write about the history of Mount Tomor, a mountain located in the south of Albania. I will quote previous and recent authors of historical books and events including recent archaeological finding. In addition, I will present ancient writings and symbols on stones and old artifacts. It is a known fact that many Albanians, western scholars, and historians have written about the mountain, starting with Albanian scholars like Jani Vreto (in his book Apology published in 1880), Konstandin Kristoforidhi (Hunter of the Mountaineer), Sami and Naim Frasheri and up to Perikli Ikonomi with (History of Tomor. Pelasgian Dodona And Tomor God of the Pelasgians, Vlora, Albania1936). Also, I will present scientific evidence from more recent researchers such as Ilir Cenollari with (Prophecies of the God of Tomor, Tirana 2009), Albert Frasheri with (Tomori, the holy mountain that we Albanians call Baba" Tirana 2015) and others. Among the authors of antiquity, I would mention Strabo, but also other authors who are quoted in his book by Perikli Ikonomi such as Homer, Polybius, Livy, Herodotus, Eskil, Pindar, Eustath, Stefan Byzanti and others (see his book page 8-12).

From western scholars, among other authors who have written about Mount Tomor is William Martin Leak with ("Travels in Northern Greece," Volume 1, London 1835). He visited Mount Tomor in person and stayed in the village of Tomor, a town with the same name as the mountain.

Also, François Pouqueville wrote the book Travels Epirus, Albania, Macedonia, and Thessaly, 1820. In his book, he talks about geographical and historical names of the Apsus River (today Osumi), Mount Tomor, and the city of Berat.

The British painter Lear wrote about Mount Tomor as well. The painter visited this area in the mid-1800s. See the book "Journals of a landscape painter in Albania, & c (1851) Edward Lear. He painted the mountain at least twice and was fascinated by its beauty.

The Italian researcher Antonio Baldacci visited the area in "ALBANIAN ITINERARIES," Rome, 1892.

The British researcher and journalist Ronald Mathews visited Mount Tomor leaving some important notes, especially about the ancient ruins near the village of Tomor, which according to him, the inhabitants of the area called it the City of Dodona.[2]

---

[2] See his book "SONS OF THE EAGLE," written by Ronald Mathews and first published in 1937, Methuen & Co.Ltd., London.

The British historian A. B. Cook has written about Tomor. He also quotes the inhabitants of the village of Tomor who call the ancient ruins at the foot of this mountain where Tomor Castle has located - the name "Dodona City". For more, see; Arthur Bernard Cook (Zeus: A Study in Ancient Religion). Cambridge University, London, 1940.

Another western author who has written about this mountain is Edwin E. Jacques in his book, "The Albanians: An Ethnic History from Prehistoric Times to the Present."

A study of the Pelasgians entitled "The Pelasgians and Their Modern Descendants," published by the University of London, 1892 by the British Historian Sir P. Colquhoun and co-author Vasso Pasha, reveal facts about the mountain. The authors call it the mountain of Zeus.

But an influential study of this area and Mount Tomor was made by the former Greek Consul in Berat (1907), Emmanuel Rikaki. [3]

In his book, Rikaki thinks that the Oracle of Dodona is not close to Ioannina, a site discovered by the Greek jurist from Arta, Constantin Carapanos. He was part of archeological expeditions who assisted him to Epirus, Thessaly, and Macedonia.

The French archaeologist William Waddington, later Prime Minister of France, led an archaeological expedition. According to various historians of antiquity, the oracle – is located on Mount Tomor near Berat. In addition, they mention the mountain under the name Tomarus. A crucial archeological

---

[3] See his book entitled "ΒΕΡΑΤΙΟΝ ΙΣΤΟΡΙΚΗ, ΑΡΧΑΙΟΛΟΓΙΚΗ ΚΑΙ ΛΑΟΓΡΑΦΙΚΗ ΠΡΑΓΜΑΤΕΙΑ ΤΟΥ ΤΜΗΜΑΤΟΣ ΒΕΡΑΤΙΟΥ" ("History, Archeology, and Folklore for Berat"), published in Athens 1910.

fact when exploring Mount Tomor, is the so-called "Dodona of Ioannina" of Costantin Carapanos.

Costantin Carapanos was not from Arta, his last name was not Carapanos but Stamou. His family emigrated from Acarnania (Aetolia) in 1822 after his grandfather was persecuted by the Sultan and exiled to Ioannina and Arta (See the book "Men of the State of Epirus" by Nicolaus B. Patcilis, Ioannina 1959, page 4 -10). Its origin is unclear, although Kosovo's academic Fehmi Agani defines it as Vlach-Greek. (see the book "Voice of intelligence for the national cause" published in Prishtina in 1995, page 94).

Carapanos was born in Arte in 1840, while the city was under Ottoman rule. He attended school in Ioannina, then studied law at the University of Athens (He was not an archaeologist nor a historian). His father worked as a supervisor in the estate of Moustafa Naili Pasha in 1859. It is thought that from Pasha's interventions, Carapanos was appointed attaché for the Turkish embassy in Paris.

At the age of 22, Carapanos went to Istanbul, and there he fell in love and married the daughter of a powerful banker from the Qesarat of Albania, Kristaq Zeografos. Zeografos, at this time, he held many public jobs in the Ottoman Empire and was the owner of the most prominent bank of the time, "Societe Generale de l'Empire Ottoman." During this period, Carapanos became the originator and sponsor of the opening of Greek community schools under the Ottoman Empire by donating books and opening new schools. In 1876, he was elected attaché to the embassy of the Ottoman Empire in Paris. During this time, he strengthened his friendship with the Prime Minister of France, William Waddington, and the Republican Leon Gambetta, two of the ardent partisans defending the Greek cause and the annexation of Epirus by Greece to the Congress of Berlin two years later, in 1878.

According to Fehmi Agani, an academic from Kosovo:

"Greece played the card of archeology in the Congress of Berlin. The idea of this movement, which turned out to be quite successful, was given by the Vlach-Greek merchant from Arta, Costandin Carapanos, (with honest and dishonest ways) as expressed at that time by Deputy. French Consul and Janines Moreau. During his stay in Paris for several years, the merchant from Arta, agent for the Greek Foreign Ministry, met Lord Waddington and Gambetta..."

William Waddington later became one of the leaders of the Congress of Berlin (1878). He was also a member of the French Academy of Sciences. He supported and helped Consantin Carapanos to defend his research work before this academy, through which he defended the idea that the Oracle of Dodona was close to Ioannina. It is no coincidence that his book entitled" "Dodone et Ses Ruines" was published in 1878, years when the Congress of Berlin was in progress. This connection between Carapanos and Waddington-Gambetta is on the official website that talks about his life at the National Archaeological Museum of Athens, where, among other things, it is stated that:

"However, to see more about this "Archaeological Intrigue," read the book in the National Library in Tirana, Albania, entitled: "REPORT OF THE DEPUTY CONSUL OF FRANCE MOREAU FOR THE FOREIGN MINISTER OF FRANCE" Volume I, 1978, pages 243-244"

"...After 1873, he invested in Greece. In 1876, when he settled in Paris, he relied upon his friendship with William Waddington who served as prime minister and foreign minister of France and Leon Gambetta, leader of the Republicans and President of the French Parliament, both of whom were also classicists, and defended Greek national affairs and above all, to press for the annexation of Epirus to Greece within the frame of the Congress in Berlin in 1878. Carapanos then became a minister in three short-lived administrations of Theodoros Diligiannis (in 1890, 1902, 1904) and founded his own party..."

The use of "archeology" for political purposes is also confirmed by the protocols and discussions held at the Berlin Congress (1978). The Congress held its proceedings from 13 June - 13 July 1878. It was a diplomatic meeting between the powers of the time (Russia, Germany, France, Great Britain, Austria-Hungary, Italy, the Ottoman Empire, and four Balkan states, Greece, Serbia, Montenegro, and Romania). It should be noted that the Balkan states did not have the right to vote. But it is known that Russia protected the interests of Serbia and Montenegro. At the same time, to protect the interests of Greece was the Prime Minister of France, William Waddington, a member of this Congress, former head of the archeological mission for Greece-Thessaly, Epirus, and Macedonia, also a member of the French Academy of Sciences. Waddington was a sponsor, a facilitator, and an advocate of Constantin Carapanos. He helped him publish his book with the title; Dodone et Ses Ruines).

The purpose of the Congress was to determine the borders of the Balkan states after the war between the Turkish Empire and Russia, (1877-1878) where Russia won this war. The book "Dodone et ses Ruines" was published at the time of the "Berlin Congress". [4] The author at the time was working at the Turkish Consulate in Paris. The book was a publication with artifacts and ancient writings (ordinances) found by Carapanos during the mission of archeology for Greece, Epirus, Thessaly, and Macedonia. The intention was for this "evidence" to be used for political purposes and territorial

---

[4] Year of publication 1878, place of publication Paris, France. Printed by "Georges Chamerot" Typography, 19 Run Saint Peres, 19.

expansion by Greece and its supporters within Congress. To this end, the Prime Minister of France (Waddington), on July 5, 1878, asked to speak to make a statement. This statement is in Protocol No. 13. Session of July 5, 1878. Parties present at the conference were respectively:

Representing Germany- The Prince of Bismarck, M. de Bülow, the Prince of Hohenlohe-Schillingsfürst.

Representing Austria-Hungary -Count Andrássy, Count Karolyi, the Baron de Haymerle.

Representing France- Mr. Waddington - The Count of Saint-Vallier. Mr. Desprez.

Representing Great Britain - The Earl of Beaconsfield, The Marquess of Salisbury, Lord Odo Russell.

Representing Italy-Count Corti. The Count of Launay.

Representing Russia-Prince Gortchacow, Count Schouvaloff, M. d'Oubril.

Representing Turkey-Alexandre Carathéodory Pasha. Mehemed Ali Pasha, Sadoullah Ber.[5]

Among these interests, those of the Hellenic background are of major importance. The Congress invited the Sublime Porte to come to an agreement with Greece for a rectification of the borders in Thessaly and Epirus and believed that this rectification could follow the Valley of Salamyrias (ancient Peneus) on the slope of the Aegean Sea and that of Kalamas on the side of the Ionian Sea.

---

[5] (see the book; "Correspondence Relating to the Congress of Berlin: With the Protocols of the Congress," By Great Britain. Foreign Office, London 1878, page 194-195).

"Congress is confident that interested parties will be able to reach an agreement. However, the Powers are ready to offer direct mediation to both parties."

According to Waddington, Greece could not thrive under the territorial conditions imposed upon her - above all, without the Gulfs of Arta and Volo, with the territories adjacent to them. Waddington finally closed his statement with a request for negotiations between Greece and Turkey on Epirus and Thessaly, using the history and archeology charter. However, he does not say anything about the Albanians who were in Epirus or their history. Albanians in this Congress were not represented; their voice was not heard. Waddington appears to have used recent archaeological discoveries for territorial and political purposes.

Carapanos presented the artifacts and pillars found in Ioannina, as artifacts of Dodona. He needed to show as pillars of a Hellenic border set according to him 3000 years ago. Therefore, his "friend" Constantin Carapanos hastened to present the ruins near the city of Ioannina and the artifacts found there as artifacts where the Oracle of Dodona once stood. According to them, it was the center of Greek civilization, but in fact was the center of Pelasgian civilization. Dodona is first mentioned in Homer's Iliad as the Pelasgian Dodona; Iliad Achilles prays to "High Zeus, Lord of Dodona, Pelasgian, living afar off, brooding over wintry Dodona" (Iliad- Homer 750 BCE). Dodona is also called not Greek, according to the geographer Meletios (page 214) quoted by the historian Perikli Ikonomi p. 9; Who says that: "Archaeological excavations have been carried out by Greek archaeologists such as Sotiris Dakaris, the author of the book "Dodona" (1994), and archaeologist Ioulia Vokotopoulou..."

"Pigeon (Pelje) were called the women of the temple who were barbarians (of non-Greek language)", in what is known today as the Oracle of Dodona near Ioannina. Carapanos explored the zone with the help of the Archaeological Mission for Greece, Thessaly, Epirus, and Macedonia (a mission led by the former French archaeologist William Waddington), in 1877-1878. In addition, many books and works have been written about the subject. However, all the artifacts found were not more than 2600 years old, around the time Homer wrote the Iliad in the VIII century BC. However, a more precise explanation is given by the co-authors Altin Kocaqi (historian) and the researcher Besim Dervishi in their article entitled "Albanians Pray in the Shadow of Tomor for the Sign of God," published on June 20, 2015, on the portal "Iliriatv.com.

Here is what co-author Altin Kocaqi writes in this article:

"... The data of antiquity should be taken only as data; as a result, they do not constitute science but are necessary for us to complete all knowledge. Therefore we are starting from these data, and precisely from Homer, Iliad II, 748-750 regarding the Ancient authors in the publication of the Academy of Sciences. Here Homer says: "Guneu from Kyfi brought 22 ships. He was followed by the tribes of the warlike Indians and Prebebs, who live in wintry Dodona..."

According to Homer, around Dodona lived the Enian tribes and those Prebebs. According to Plutarch In his book "The Parallel Lives" (1. V, 19 1. VI, 21, VIII, 4 and IX, 6) quoted by Perikli Ikonomi on pages 9 and 10 of his book "History of Tomor, Pelasgian Dodona And Tomor God of the Pelasgians", the tribes that lived near the Oracle of Dodona, were Select, Enians, Orestes , Prevejte and Athamanet. Hence, Athamanet and Prevejte were expelled from here by Lapith, the great-grandparents of today's "labe" (Area that this name knows today in Vlora-Tepelena).

Before I discuss the two tribes located nearby Dodona, I want to quote former Greek Consul in Berat (1907), Emmanuel Rikaki, in his book "ΒΕΡΑΤΙΟΝ ΙΣΤΟΡΙΚΗ, ΑΡΧΑΙΟΛΟΓΙΚΗ ΚΑΙ ΛΑΟΓΡΑΦΙΚΗ ΠΡΑΓΜΑΤΕΙΑ ΤΟΥ ΤΜΗΜΑΤΟΣ ΒΕΡΑΤΙΟΥ" (History, Archeology, and Folklore for Berat), published in Athens 1910:

Furthermore, I want to explain to the reader that from the book and his study, I will dismiss the nationalist claims he has made about Berat and the area surrounding the city. Instead, I want to present only the historical and scientific evidence he offers. It is understood that the 1800s and 1900s were turbulent years for the Balkan Peninsula. The last years of the Ottoman Empire the Balkan states were in a political, military, historical, and archaeological war to expand their territories at the expense of smaller nations. Therefore, I will mention only the data the author has forwarded as historical sources, the ancient authors of history. On page 6 of the book, he wrote:

"..."Η επαρχία Βερατίου κείται γεωγραφικώς εις το δευτικών μέρος της Ιλλυρικής ή Μακεδονικής χώρας, εκαλείτο δε το πάλαι Ελλοπία (κατά τον Ησίοδον)...."

Translation: The province of Berat geographically coverage in the western part of the Illyrian or Macedonian country was called old Ellopia (according to Hesiod).

It is interesting that Rikaki quotes the ancient author Hesiod and calls the area around Berat by the name of old Hellopia. The book "Illyrians and Ancient Authors," co-authored by Frano Prendi, Hasan Ceka, Selim Islami, and Skender Anamali, as well as translators of Greek-Latin texts, Sotir Papakristo, Stefan Prifti, Pashko Geci Henrik Lacaj, Kole Shiroka, and Koco Bozhori (Year of publication Prishtina, Kosovo 1979, printing house "Rilindja" p. 161) - states that:

"...It is a place that Hesiod says is called Hello with fields, and at the swamp at the bottom of it, is Dodona. Some think that this shrine was called so by the swamps. But Apollodorus says that near the net, a river called Seleent, and the inhabitants were not called Helle but Selle, "Away from Eyfyres and the river Seleneet." Skepsi says it is not about the EYFYREN OF THESPROTIS but about ELEJTE. There is the Seleneet River while there are none in Thesprotia or Molossia...." Interestingly, these authors (see also page 161) quote Strabo in his book (volume VII).

"...The oracle was earlier near Skotusa, a town in the province of Pelasgiotis. After the oak was burned by someone at the behest of APOLLO, he (the oracle) was transferred to DODONE to give messages, not with words but symbols like the oracle of Amon in Libya ...."

My note: Carapanos discovered the oracle near Ioannina. Although as it is known, there were two cities named Scotussa. Titus Livy's book "The History of Rome: The Twentieth to the Thirtieth Books, Volume 2," page 159, states that:
 "By the name Scotussa, there were two towns that held that name; one in Thessaly, the other in Macedonia. /Adam./"
 Suppose this city in Thessaly is located near Larissa, whereas in Macedonia (Illyria) is unknown exactly where it was, but it is thought to have been located near Lake Ohrid. Duplication of names makes the work of researchers even more difficult. But let us continue to quote Rikaki's book below. According to him:

"...The history of this place from ancient times to the present day is very dark. According to Thucydides, the region of Berat is inhabited by the Paranians, around the Aiantos or Aoos river (now Viosa). The Atindanes lived between Aoos and the "Apsos river near Apollonia." The King was Tharypas, grandfather of Neoptolemus (Thucydides, Book B Chapter

SO). Orestiada (now Berat) is located on the right side of the "Apsos River," which flows west and ten hours away from the Adriatic Sea in the village of Seman…"

Rikaki in this passage, has shown us that Berat is called Orestia; he also explains why this name was attributed to the city.

The scholar Perikli Ikonomi in his book on the history of Mount Tomor (1936), on page 23, mentions some names of this city. He says that; Berat, as a city in its province, had six names Orestia, Lefki Petra (White Stone), Antipatra, Pulheriopoie, Beligrad, Berat. Unfortunately, however, the ancient name of Berat has not been found by archaeologists.

On page 6 of his book, Rikki says that; Antipitrei, probably opposite to it, summoned Orestias was another city called Patras. In his book (see page 6), Rikki wrote that in Berat (castle), a resident handed over to the local authorities a stone with ancient writing. On this stone were old writing and the head of a woman and a man.

"ΚΟΣΜΗCΕΝ ΜΕ ΦΙ ΛΟΣ ΠΑΤΡωΙΟΣ Η ΔΕ ΠΑΤΡΙC ΜΟΙ ΠΑΤΡΑΙ ΑΤΑΡΚΑΤΕχω ΓΥΛΑ ΚΙΟΝ ΠΕΔΙΟΝ."

According to him, the city of Orestias was then called Antipatrea; perhaps opposite to it was another city called Patras. Its stone was found in a Christian house and handed over to the local administration. But ANTIPATRA is an old name that some consider a Greek name, some Latin, but in fact, it is Albanian. It has nothing to do with Greek or the name of the Macedonian general Antipatra, a significant name. "Anti" - opposite of, and Patra - meaning Baba (father) - shrine - oracle. This is the city in front of the shrine of Tomor. And it is known that the city of Berat is located in front of Mount Tomor. The mountain that the ancient Albanians called Baba Tomori was the ancient oracle to whom they confessed or consulted. For this stone, we have data in the book "Schriften der Balkankommission, Antiquarische Abteilung," Published: in Wien: Alfred Hölder, 1900, pages 193. On this page is the picture of the stone with the old writings.

This photograph is in the book "Schriften der Balkankommission, Antiquarische Abteilung", page 139.

The stone is thought to have been found in the basements of Andrea Salabanda's house, and was handed over by the owner to the local administration. The stone has been in the house for a long time, but it is thought that he was taken to Pojan, Fier (Apolonia). Although Rikki and Perikli Ikonomi have given various names for Berat, which are based on the data of Titus Livy and Polybius as well as other authors. Archaeologist Hasan Ceka thought that Berat had another name in Illyria. He thought that Antipatra was not Berat. According to him, in the book XXIX 12 of Livy, the conditions of peace between the Romans and the Macedonians were like this: The

Parthians, Dimalas, Barguli, and Eugene belonged to the Romans, while the Atintans belonged to the Macedonians.

In this agreement, according to him, it is clear that there is no word for Dasaria, Antipatra, or other cities of this tribe. The city of Antipatrea is not mentioned in this agreement. If Antipatra was where Berat is today, it would definitely have been mentioned by Livy. Archaeologist Hasan Ceka thought that the city of Berat was the Illyrian Barguli. On page 21 of his study entitled "Notes from the historical geography of Southern Illyria," published in the Magazine "Iliria" Number 1 Tirana 1984 (From page 15 to page 26), Hasan Ceka wrote:

"...N. Pajakowski, «Starozytny Epir i jego mieszkancy» Poznan 1970, p. 92, derived from the name, locates Barguli in the village of Bargulas in Berat. This is also the opinion of S. Islami (Illyrian State in the War Against Rome, Iliria Magazine number III, 1974 p. 23, note 97), who places the ancient city of Bargullas in the village of Bargullas.

Archaeologist Neritan Ceka (La Viile Illyrienne de la Basse - Selce, Iliria II 1972, p. 97/8) thinks that Barguli was where the Berat Castle is located. Bargulium of Livy could very well identify with Berat if, from the etymological and semantic point of view, it was related to the Albanian Bardhyl. The Slavic name Belgrade, Belgrade (white city) by which this city was known in the Middle Ages would thus have its explanation. As for Bargulas, this would be a foundation carried out later by the inhabitants of the ancient city...."

Archaeologists such as Hasan Ceka and Neritan Ceka thought that the city of Bargul (Bagulum) mentioned by Livy may have been in Berat. However, the possibility is not ruled out that he was in the village of Bargullas near Mount Tomor at the place that today is known as "Koroni Castle." Here is what the historian and researcher Altin Kocaqi wrote, describing an expedition to this village (Bargullas) of the place called "Koroni Castle":

"... On the way back, we accidentally stumbled upon broken and scattered pottery when quite by chance, the scholar Valter Koxhaj turned his eyes to 'one of the symbols spiritually connected for a long time: the symbol of the Pelasgian Sun, with eight rays, which has accompanied the world of 'Pelasgian actors' for centuries…." [6]

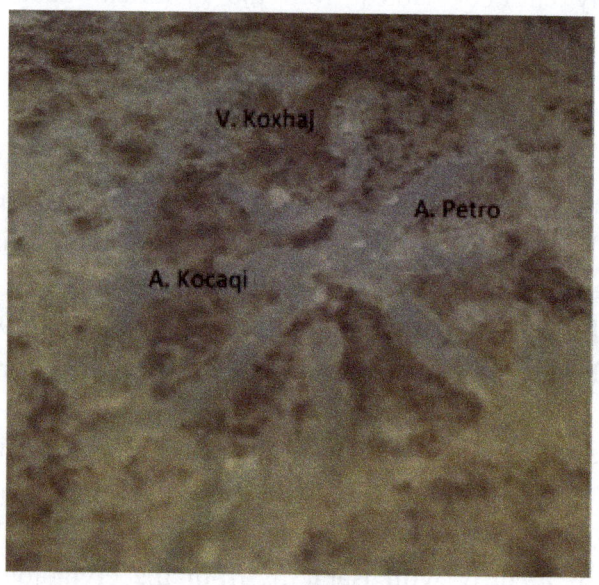

Photo of the Pelasgian Sun or "Star" found in the village of Bargullas by researchers and historians Altin Kocaqi, Valter Koxhaj, and A. Petro. Bargullas village, Berat Albania. August 21, 2016

---

[6](See; Article "Gjurmë pellazgjike në Tomor. Simboli i Diellit Pellazgjik"(Pelasgian traces in Tomor. Symbol of the Pelasgian Sun) - Altin Kocaqi. Published on the Portal "Dodonanews.Net" on November 5, 2017. With the permission of the researcher Valter Koxhaj. Or search for this link: "https://dodonanews.net/gjurme-pellazgjike-ne-tomor-simboli-diellit-pellazgjik-altin-kocaqi/?fbclid=IwAR1LdzVGNOI5oRBm2MVGHzV9pV_ww6DDPjd0)

In his work, Neritan Ceka says that Bargul means Bardhyl, which translates into "White Star." This name was also held by the First King of Illyria Bardhyli. But the name Bargul has other meanings. "Bardh-Gur" or White Stone. It is known that the houses and buildings of the city of Berat are built with a type of white stone which is mostly found in the area. And the name given to the Slavs later during their invasions was Belgrade which means "White City." Hence, finding the symbol of the Sun in this area was key to justify the name Ilion. The name of the city "Ilion," in Albanian means "Star" or "Sun."

There is strong archaeological evidence that leads to the conclusion that this area was the city of the sun or the star. It is known that the name Ilion or in Latin Ilium, is called Troy. According to historian Arthur B. Cook: "Zeus is called the god of heaven, the god of light. But he is also identified with the Sun. The Iliad thus describes the crash of a battle between Argives and Trojans: The din of both rose to the upper sky and the rays of Zeus.[7]

About 400 A.D. Macrobius, an equally enthusiastic advocate of the solar cult, devotes a whole chapter to proving that Zeus must be the Sun. Ioannes Laurentius, the Lydian, in his work on the Roman calendar, which was written in the early part of the sixth century, repeatedly takes that view. And Eustathios, archbishop of Thessalonike, who lived during the later half of the twelfth century, does the same in his learned commentary on the Iliad and Odyssey. [8] These authors and others like them attempt to justify their opinion by citing certain passages from Homer. [9] The cult of the Sun has

---

[7] (Iliada I 3. 837). Cp. Eustath. in II. p. 962, 64 f. Eustathi thought that Zeus sometimes means' the Sun

[8] (see Eustath. in II. pp. 40, 29, 128, i4ff., 728, 16, id. in Od. pp. 1387, 26, 1713, 14 f., 1726, 61

[9] (see; Il. 1. 423 f, Il. Hesiod, Orpheus, Pherekydes, Sophokles, and Platon. (See book; Zeus: a study in ancient religion, Cook, Arthur

been identified with Zeus; the same cult has been identified in Egypt with the god Serapis, who wears a bull skull on his head. Later after the entry of Christianity, Zeus was superseded by Saint Elias. Saint Elias represents not only the mountain Zeus but Helios.[10]

The word Elia comes from the word Ilio, Ilion, Ylli (Star- Sun in the Albanian language). Where there was a shrine dedicated to Zeus-Sun, there, a Christian church was erected, which was dedicated to Saint Elias. I will discuss this below to present archaeological facts and historical sources where the shrine of Zeus - the Sun was built on Mount Tomor. The area where the Church of St. Elias was built is at the peak of Mount Tomor. It is thought that in the same area, the ancient city of Ilion may have been located.

We will present the symbols of the Sun and the Star discovered in stones and old artifacts.

How did the worship of the cult of Zeus pass from paganism to Christianity and today in the Bektashi order?

The priests of Dodona worshiped the cult of the Sun but also the Star Sirio. Enzo Gati, in the book GLI ETRUSCHI (Rome 1979) page 153 says that on Mount Pore located in southern Italy (at the top of the boot), were found Etruscan writings, a prayer, where the writer addresses the god EA and SIRIO. It is known that God EA was the god of the Illyrians. But even Ylli Sirio was worshiped by them. This star is found in the Dog Constellation. It is 20 times brighter than the Sun and bigger. It is called SUN AFTER SUN. The Sirio star is a Star that has the color white. For this reason, the first king of the Illyrians, Bardhyli, was named this name to honor this Star.

Bernard, Publisher Cambridge, Publication date 1914-1940, page 7, 186,187).
[10] (See, A.B.Cook page 178-179).

For this reason, in Tomor we have a city named Bardhgul that archaeologist Selim Islami has identified according to data from Titus Livy. While archaeologists Hasan and Neritan Ceka give the meaning "Yll i Bardhë," which, as we said, has the meaning "White Star," the color with which is the Sirio Star.

Researcher and historian Robert Temple, in 1976 wrote the book THE SIRIUS MYSTERY – and dedicated it to Sirio Star. However, according to scientists, there are two Sirio stars. Star A and Star B and both are white, but Star B is small and not easily distinguished. It is also called the Dwarf Star. Scientists and historians believe that Sirio was worshiped during the antiquity. If the Sun was the star that warmed and gave light to Earth, Sirio had to do with spiritual faith; in a way, it warmed the soul of humans.

I will talk in the book about the findings in the area around Mount Tomor, the findings of artifacts with the symbol of two stars. But also for old maps carved in stone. Because it is known that the priests of oracles were astrologers, they knew how to predict solar eclipses, and they also had other astrological knowledge to predict fate.

But let me quote E. Rikaki in his book, on pages 6 and 7:

"...Της Εορδής το πάλαι οι κάτοικοι θα εκαλούντο Σελλοί (πιθα νως οι νύν Σουλιοβάρ), περί ών αναφέρει ο Όμηρος (Ιλιάς Στοιχ. Π. Στίχ. 233), ποιούμενος περί της αρχικέτες Δωδιώγης, ότι έκειτο αύτη επί της κορυφής του όρους Τομόρου, εξ ου εφαίνετο η 'Αδριατική θάλασσα και εις τας πορείας του οποίου κατώκουν οι ανιπτόποδες Σελλοί. Ως φαίνεται, εις το πρής και της πόλεως Βερατίου όρος Τομόρι θα υπήρχει επίσης μαντείον αφιε ρωμένον εις τον Δία και μη έχον σχέσιν τινά προς το ανακαλυ φθέν εν τη κάτω 'Ηπείρο, αφού άλλως τε, ως γνωστόν, πολλά τοιαύτα μαντεία υπήρχαν εν τη αρχαιότητι..."

Translation: "In the past, the inhabitants of Eordi would be called Selloi (probably the current Souliovar), about which Homer (Iliada Item. P. Verse. 233). It must be said that the real Dodona was at the top of Mount Tomor. From where the Adriatic Sea could be seen, on whose slopes live the inhabitants of the area, Selloi[11]. On Mount Tomor, in the city of Berat, there would also be an oracle dedicated to Zeus, which had nothing to do with the discovery of Lower Epirus,[12] as it is known, many oracles of such have existed in antiquity...."

According to Perikli Ikonomi, Dionys Perigjitiu says that Dodona is located in an open place (see pg. 11). Also, on page 11, Perikli Ikonomit quotes Skymnos Hios (Geography 1, III, 22, VI, 6 VII, 6) who says that inside the ground (cave) lived Selloi of Dodona mixed with barbarians (non-Greek speaking inhabitants), except for the Sulova area, Rikaki and Ikonomi, thought to be the dwellings of the inhabitants of Selloi.

In this book, I will discuss the southwest of Tomor, where the village of Selan is located, which is similar to the name Selloi. In this village, there is a rock with the name "Selani Rock." Here, during 1970-1980 archaeologists discovered many artifacts from antiquity. Also, from 2015 till recently, more artifacts with historical value were located in the same area. I will elaborate more about the Sulova area, located northwest of Tomor.

In the data that Rikaki provided, the Adriatic Sea was seen from the top of Tomori, and it is in complete synchrony with the data of Aeschylus, which is quoted by P. Ikonomi. He states that: The temple of Dodona is located at the top of a high

---

[11] (my note; who walked barefoot and slept on the ground)
[12] (my note; it refers to the Oracle of Ioannina)

mountain. (Aeschylus Book VII, 8 and VIII, 3). In his book, on page 7, Rikaki wrote that:

"This possibility [13] is based on the fact that Albanians still consider this mountain as a holy place, which is called Mali Mir (good mountain), and most Muslims and especially those of the Bektashi sects of Ali (Bektashids) go to the highest peak to pray and make a sacrifice. Even today, the inhabitants have a reverence for the mountain that they call it by the name Baba Tomori (Father Tomaros) and swear by his name."

According to Rikaki, some Homeric rites are still applied in the area, such as the rite of walking barefoot (in Sulove but also in other areas), reminiscent of the priests of Dodona. He thought that in the beginning, Tomori area was populated by inhabitants who then moved, and the cities of Berat, and Apollonia were founded. He also talks about an old road discovered in the neighborhood of Berat, Uznove, which connected Tomor with Berat and Apollonia.

Hence, both Perikli Ikonomi and Emanuel Rikaki thought that areas near Tomor and Tomor mountain were the oldest provinces inhabited by Selloi, Hellet Enian and Prrebejte tribes. According to them, Mount Tomor is the mountain where Homer's Pelasgian Dodona was located.

These opinions were shared by other Albanian writers whom we have mentioned, such as Jani Vreto, Sami Frasheri, Konsandin Krtistoforidhi, but also more recent reasercher such as Ilir Cenollari, Sulejman Mato, Altin Kocaqi, Albert Frasheri, and others. While many others oppose the argument Tomori is not old, there is no archeological discovery in the area around it; there is no ancient city, no valuable artifacts have been discovered, and other claims. They say there are only legends

---

[13] (My note; that the Oracle of Dodona is located in Tomor)

and superstitions about Mount Tomor, but no archeological facts.

Opponents of the thesis that in Tomor was the oracle of Dodona connect the sanctity of this mountain only with the fact that there today is a place of worship for the Bektashi order. They do not mention any archeological sites or any names from the ancient cities around Tomor, names that have to do with the cult of the sun and the star. In addition, they do not mention that in Tomor was a pagan oracle on which a church was built and today is a shrine of the Bektashi order. They do not say that dozens of symbols are found in stones and artifacts, symbols of the sun, fish, flowers, tree of life, oak, etc., and symbols associated with distant historical eras. They do not mention where even today, the cult of the Dodona oak is worshiped. They do not mention the legendary wind (Stocenit or Stercenius), which set in motion the "Dodona Cauldrons."

In this book, I want to shed some light on the ancient sites around Tomor. I want to polish the artifacts, ancient cities, place names, and legends of this mountain. I will write about the archeological sites around it, the tales, the old cities, the ancient writings on the stones, the worship of the oak cult, and other symbols. I will bring everything to show the antiquity of this mountain, everything that serves as clue for the discovery of the Oracle of Dodona.

I was a young child there when my grandfather told me that once in the 1930s, he had met on the street a group of foreign tourists who were going to Mount Tomor. Of course, they had translators, but he could hear a word from them that impressed him and that he often told us.

It was the name "Dodona." A word he had probably heard for the first time or perhaps heard from his ancestors. My village is located at the foot of Mount Tumor in its northwestern part. The house where I was born is built of stone from this area, covered with gray stone slabs. Every morning when I woke up in front of me, I saw Tomor's brother, Shpiragu, who, according to the legend with whom he fought.

The Northern Cuka and its rocks looked like ancient Illyrian gods with long beards at first glance. I was always impressed by these rocks. They looked like sculptures, and above them flew the eagles that our area called "Larashi," a kind of giant falcon with nests on these rocks. I was also profoundly impressed by the "Stocen" wind. I usually started to feel it in the afternoon. Sometimes the wind was so strong that someone in the village showed that it had raised people and animals in the air. I was also impressed by the lightning in the summer when it rained.

They seemed to have their starting point from the top of Tomori. They were much scarier and lightened up the nights. I was thirteen when I climbed up Mount Tomor. It was January 1990, but strangely, there was no snow. My grandmother was lying in bed very sick. She was looking for snow. Although according to her superstitious grandfather, this was a bad omen, while some others said that the snow in Tomor had healing powers. I remember climbing up to the Source of Vitalem, alone at two o'clock at night. There was my first climb to Tomor alone. I found the snow and brought it home. I realized I had grown up.

After the 1990s, I went almost every year to Mount Tomori, in the southeast, usually to collect herbal tea, a very good and curative tea. These were the first contacts with the mountain. I have been reading and researching deeply about this mountain for about ten years.

Sometimes, I think I collected sufficient material. However, as soon as a new archeological find appears, or I read a new book; I still think I still have to research. Thus, I wouldn't be surprised if I published the second part of this book after a few years, and in it, you would find new facts about this mountain that may conflict with the old ones. I once read that many scholars or historians, when they have returned to their studies with new and complementary studies, have they have corrected the mistakes. The more one reads, or researches, the more one learns. Discoveries of tomorrow will probably be more important than mine. But let this book serve not as a cornerstone but as a "pebble" on the walls of the building that our ancestors and we have built, the grand Albanian history.

    I graduated in law from the Faculty of Law in Prishtina and later received a Master's degree in criminal law from the same honored University. I have investigated and research on the subject for a period of ten years or more and in this book, I want to share what I have ascertained and collected from the field, such as the legends, the names, the data from renown authors of antiquity and the contemporary ones, the archeological facts discovered, and their meaning.

BETWEEN THE LEGEND AND THE TRUTH: FROM PAGANISM TO CHRISTIANITY TO OUR DAYS

Photo by Artur Guni. The circular structure of the stone at the northern top of Tomor (HEIGHT 2416 m).

The circular structure could have been used as energy generating devices. According Robert Elsie but and F. W.Hasluck, Osman Myderrizi, Jozef Swire, and according to the Bektashi believers, Abaz Aliu has the tomb on the high peak of Mount Tomor, and is visited there by pilgrims:

"...Being a few hundred meters above the Bektashi tekke which was built there in 1916, and is currently run by Baba Shabani. The place is visited every year from 20 to 25 August and thousands of sheep are sacrificed. According to the legend, Abas Aliu was half-brother with Hasan and Hussein (brothers) and he was originally from Arabia and came on a white horse to protect the country from barbarians. He is thought to have passed five days in the mountain of Tomor before he left to live in the Mount Olympus.... He returns every year for five days, therefore in the month of August the Pilgrimage lasts only five days. The Albanian poet Naim Frasheri .... says that Haxhi Bektashi, the prophet of the Bektashis, was watching the Christian believers ascend to Mount tomor on 15 August to honor the Virgin Mary.[14]

Another legend is told by the German Albanologist Maximilian Lambertz.

"...Baba Tomori is married to the Beauty of the Earth. She spends the whole day with her sister, The Beauty of The Sea. Tomor Mountain looks up to the castle of Berat, which this older man jealously guards as his most precious gene. Above the valley is the Shpirag mountain, with wrinkles formed by powerful water streams descending to its flat and steep sides."

Baba Tomor has taken the Earthly Beauty to be his bride. She spends her days with her sister, the Sea Beauty, but when evening comes, the wind, a faithful servant of Baba Tomor, carries her back up the mountainside to him. Mount Tomor overlooks the town of Berat, which the old man jealously guards as his favorite city. Across the valley is Mount Shpirag, with furrow-like torrents of water running down its slopes. While Baba Tomor was dallying in bed with the Earthly Beauty one day, Shpirag took advantage of the moment and

---

[14] (Page 3. book "A Dictionary of Albanian Religion, Mythology, and Folk Culture" Robert Elsie. Published in USA 2001)

advanced to take over Berat. The four guardian eagles duly awakened Baba Tomor from his dreams. When told of Shpirag's surreptitious plans, Baba Tomor arose from his bed. His first concern was for the Earthly Beauty's safety, so he ordered the East Wind to carry her back to her sister's home. Mounting his mule, Tomor then set off to the battle with Shpirag. With his scythe, Tomor lashed into Shpirag, inflicting upon him many wounds that can be seen today as the furrows running down the mountainside. A trace of the hoof of Baba Tomor's mule can, it is said, be seen near the village of Sinja. Shpirag, for his part, pounded Tomor with his cudgel and left many a wound on the lofty mountain. The two giants ultimately slew one another, and the maiden drowned in her tears, which became the Osum river.[15] Another testimony is that of Joseph Swire in King Zog's Albania, London 1937 p.253; he gives the local legend:

"...On August 25, a long time ago... Abas Ali came from Arabia to Berat, and mounting a great white horse (which has left hoof-marks upon the mountain), he fought the barbarians of the neighborhood. When he had overcome them, he rested for five days on Tomori, then went to dwell on Mount Olympus; but every year, he returns on August 25 for five days, when there come Bektashis and Christians too, sometimes eight or nine thousand people, to pay him homage. First, they bring their sheep for food, slaughter them on the summit, then take them down to their bivouacs by the tekke...."

Ronald Matthews in his book Sons of the Eagle wrote the same legend, but with a few changes. [16]

---

[15] / MAXIMILIAN LAMBERTZ "die mithologye der albane" shtutgard 1973 p. 504-505 /. Taken from the author PIRO TASE in his book "FOREIGNERS FOR ALBANIA" Second Edition, USA 2010, pp. 15-16. Translated into English by albanologist Robert Elsie. Web page; "Albanian Literature in Translation" Robert Elsie or https://albanianhistory.org/albanianliterature/oral_lit3/OL3-01.html /

"Many hundreds of years ago...there were two brothers, very holy men, who lived in Arabia. One day they arrived in Albania: No one knows how, some say through the air. The younger of the two set up his house in Berat, where he was highly revered for his sanctity and became the town's patron saint. But the elder brother, Ali, was a great warrior. Throughout the countryside, he rode on his wonderful horse, challenging and conquering the barbarians who lived around. His horse could cover miles in a single bound. You may still see the marks of its hooves on the rocks of Tomori... Then, at last, a day came when Ali had overcome all his enemies. So, he retired to the summit of Tomori, where the shrine stands today. For three days, he meditated alone on the fate of his foes and the future of his country, Albania. Then one last time, he vaulted into the saddle of his great horse. Through the air, it bore him to the top of Mount Olympus in Greece, and there he lived forever... But every year, on August 15, Christians and Moslems make their pilgrimage every year and for three days offer sacrifices at the shrine...."

The reader can find both legends in the book written by Arthur Bernard Cook, "Zeus: a study in ancient religion: Zeus god of the dark sky (earthquake, clouds, wind, dew, rain, meteorites), p. 68, 69 and 70, Cambridge, 1940.

But Ronald Mathews had written another legend in his book Sons of the Eagle, p 269 and 270 in the chapter City on a Hill, London 1937.

"... Long ago, that was before men could remember, and it had at that time a lofty peak, like Tomor itself, of which it was inordinately vain. One day, it cried across the valley: 'I am the lord of Albania, Tomori, and not you. Give up your throne to me.' And it hurled great rocks through the air at its rival: we could see the marks they made there to this day. But a little

---

[16] p. 273, in the chapter A Mountian of Zeus, London 1937

matter of bombardment with rocks, even though they weighed twenty tons apiece, would not make any difference to Baba Tomori. So he said nothing; he drew his sword and, with one blow, struck off the mountain's head; the old caretaker declared that it was as flat as you see it today. And then with terrible rage, he carved those gullies all down his challenger's face, that men might see the marks and know who is lord in Albania...."

Again in this book, on pages 276 and 277, Ronald Mathews gives us another version of the legend:

"... But both gendarmes now wanted to interpose their own versions of how Ali came to reside on top of Tomori. Their stories were markedly irreverent to the holy man and very much in line with the reputed character of the Father of God. What it amounted to, was that Ali's brother, the saint, had been a tradesman in Berat. Ali had been in the habit of visiting him very frequently and discussing matters of high philosophy cross-legged on the floor of his shop. One day the brother had to go out on an errand. Returning unexpectedly, he was confronted, shocked, and amazed by the real reason for these frequent visits. Ali was making furious and very successful love to his girl servant. "Go," the saint thundered, "and never enter Berat again. Go back to your mountain home, which you ought never to have left. For if I ever see you here again. I shall not only denounce you before all people, but I shall very probably kill you.' So Ali returned to Tomori and lived there to this day...."

According to the old resident of Sinje village, Kristofor Mjeshtri. At the entrance of Sinje village near to the place which is now called "Tunnels." It was a place which was called" Horse Footprint" or "Mule Footprint." There was a horseshoe stamped in stone. But the rock was destroyed when the local road was built. This happened before the '90s.

Photo by Sofokli Mjeshtri. Sinje, Berat.

Kristofor Mjeshtri is near the place called "Horse Footprint." It was located near the second hole on the road. In this village was found by Mr. S. Mjeshtri, a carved stone that resembles a human foot or footprint.

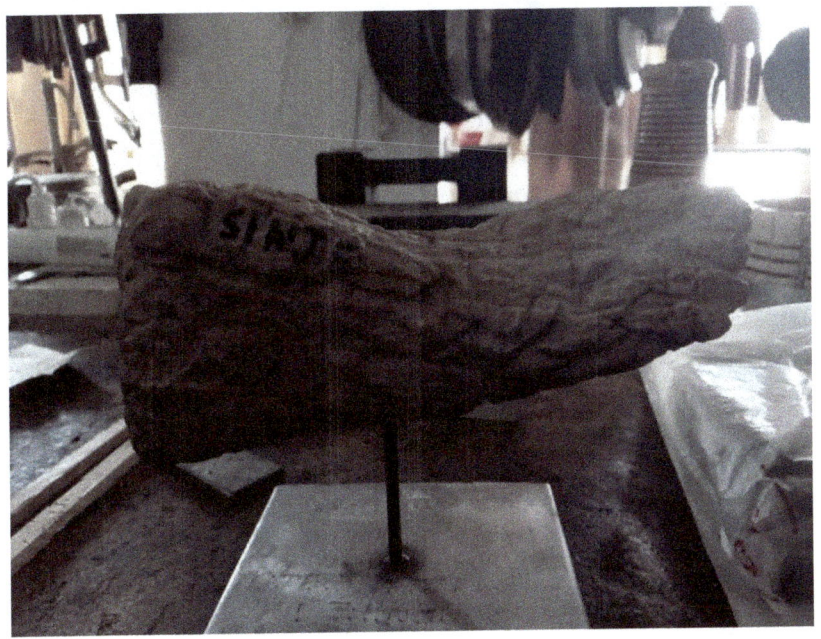

Photo by Besim Dervishi. Polican 2021. Object found by Sofokli Mjeshtri in the place called "Bregu i Zhapes," Sinje, Shpiragu Mountain, 2007

Photo by Besim Dervishi. Polican 2021. Found by Sofokli Mjeshtri in the place called "Bregu i Zhapes", Sinje, Shpirag Mountain, 2007

But the most popular places where they are located are the Horse Footprint are in Tomor Mount, Dhores Village. These footprints are also called "The Footprints of Abaz Ali." A footprint is found near the village of Dhores, 7km from Corovod city. Another is found in the place called "Taronin" Cepan Mount, Skrapare. Another is in Prishta Village Skrapar, and another is in Bargulias Village. A long time ago, these were called "FOOTPRINTS OF GOD."

Photo by Rajmonda Bala, Mount Tomor (Kulmak) August 2022 Albania.

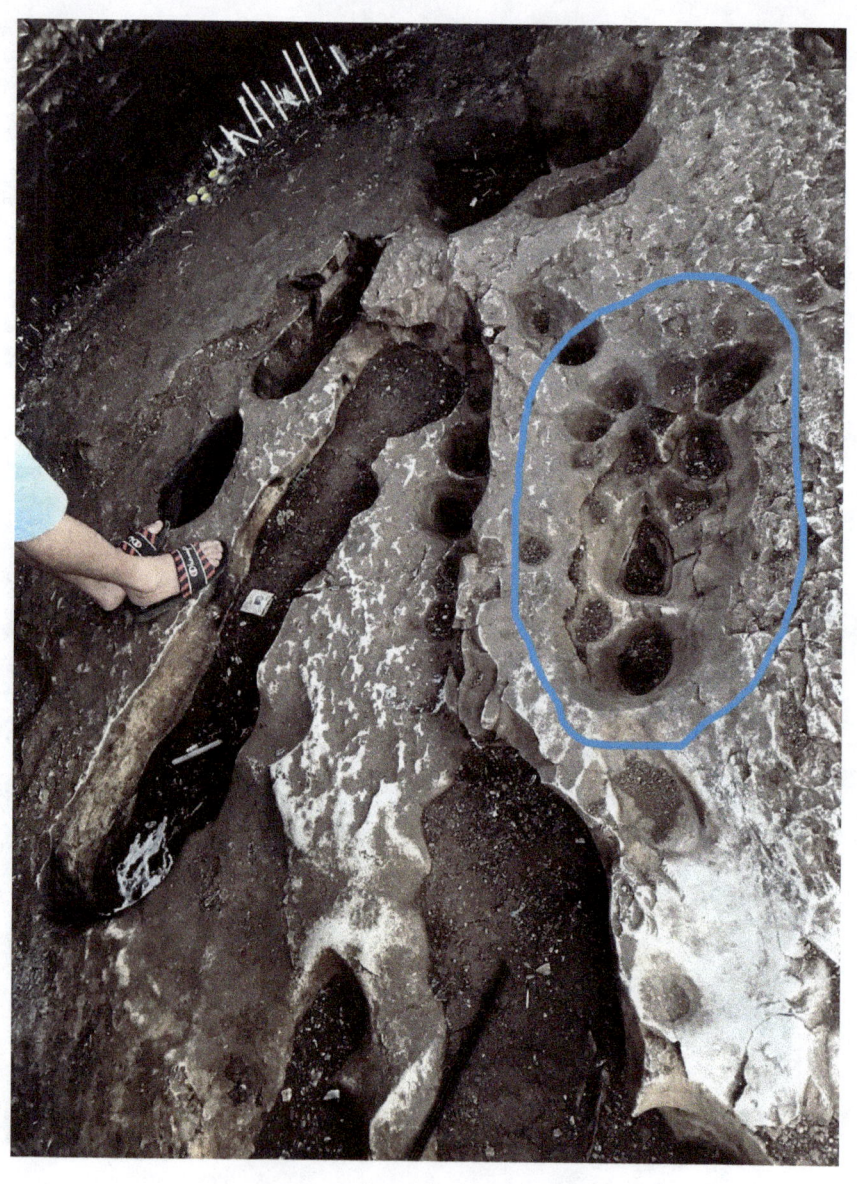

Photo by Rajmonda Bala, Mount Tomor (Kulmak) August 2022 Albania.

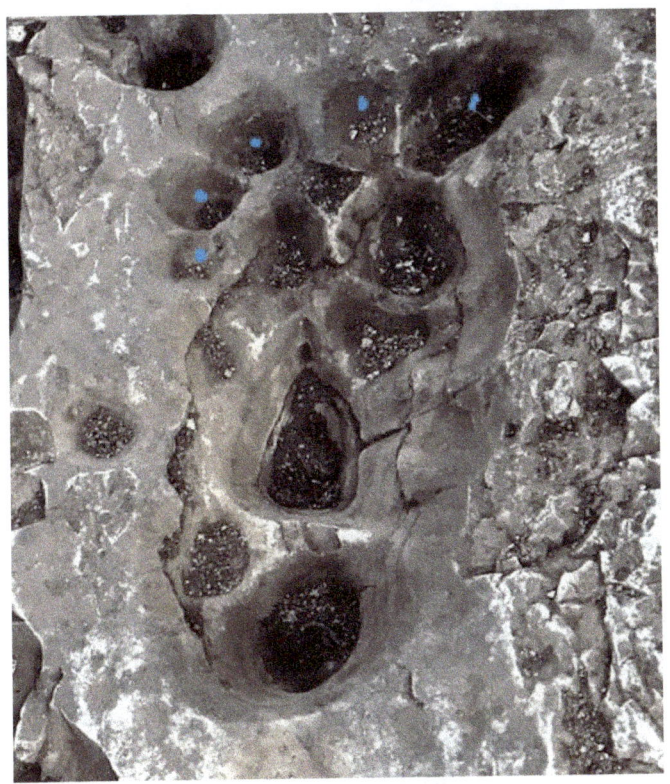

Photo by Rajmonda Bala, Mount Tomor (Kulmak) August 2022 Albania.

The place is called "Footprint" in the southern part of Mount Tomor. Today this place is known by the name "Footprint of Abaz Ali," but in the old times, this place was known by the name "Footprint of the God." "Footprint in the shape of a human foot." Photos were taken by Rajmonda Bala, Mount Tomor (Kulmak) August 2022 Albania.

Photo by Besim Dervishi, 2021. Horse Footprint, Dhores Village.

The Legend of Abaz Aliu says:

"Abaz Aliu came to Mt. Tomor from Qerbelaja upon his white horse to defeat his enemies. It is suggested that Abaz Aliu left a footprint on the stone in Dhores (above the Canyons) from where he flew to Mount Tomorr to defeat his enemies and left an imprint on the rock on this mount."

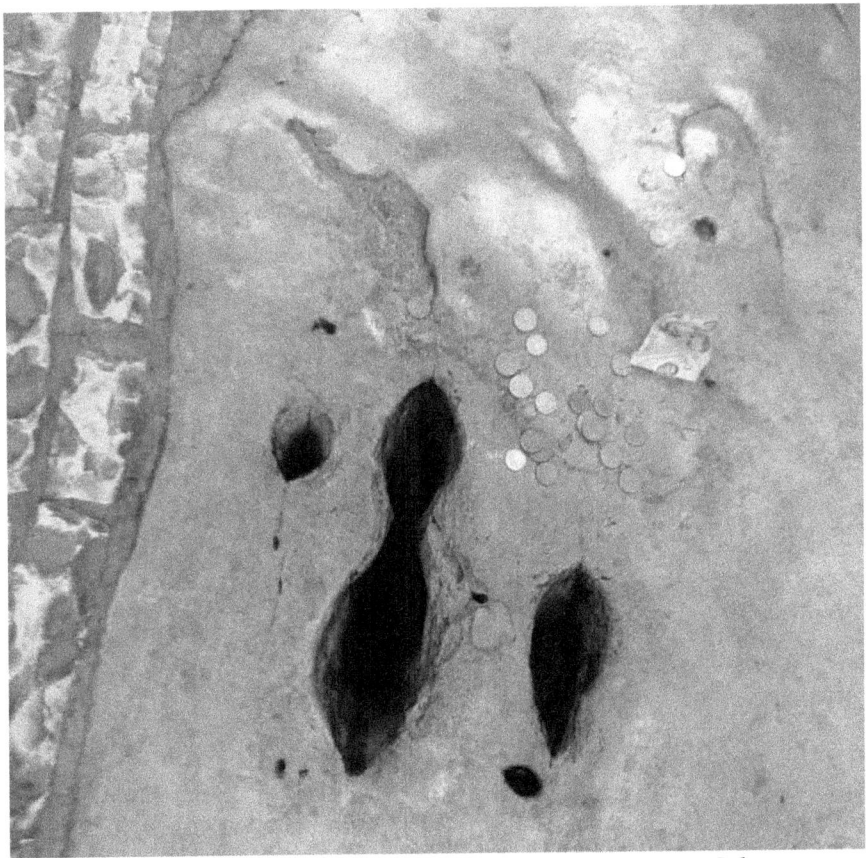

Photo by Besim Dervishi, 2021. Horse Footprint, Dhores Village. Albania 2021

This legend has several theories, but the most reliable is the oldest.

In these photos are two coins which were found near the place called "Pelasgian Stones". At the entrance of "Terova" Cave. Places that are called "Pelasgian Stones" and "Terova Cave" are located northeast of Mount Tomor. Photo of the first coin. Both sides. Photo taken by Kadri Talaj.

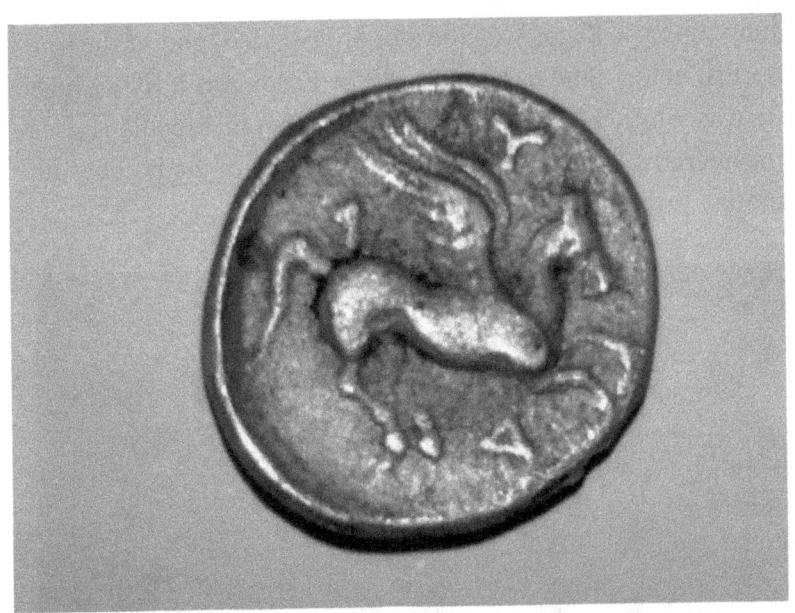

Photo of the second coin. Both sides. Photo by Kadri Talaj.
Ancient Coins of Illyria city of Dyrrha (Today Durresi). Head of Hercules wearing lion-skin headdress. On the other side of the coin are Pegasus flying and two letters. The letter "Y" is the initial of "Ylliria" and the letter "D" is the initial of "Dyrrahu".

In mythology, Pagas was the son of Poseidon, god of the sea, storms, horses, and earthquakes. The Pegas was a flying horse. He was white. Even today, the white horse in Albania is considered a lucky sign. Again, the symbol of the horse is in another artifact found in the Tomor area.

Photo published by Nori Pelivani. Polican 2021

Photo published by Nori Pelivani. Polican 2021

    The circle where are two horses, according to some historians it's a representation of heaven and earth. The small circle symbolizes the sky and the sun. According A. B. Cook this is the chapel of St. Elias. In the beginning, the circle of stones was a pagan shrine; then it turned into a Christian church. Today it is a Bektashi shrine. According to Robert Elsie [17]

".. Saint Elias, Albanian Shëndelli, Shën Ilija, or Shën Li - Romanian Santilie, Aromunian Sândâliya, "indiliya, Serbocr. Ilija, initially the Old Testament prophet Elijah, rides through the heavens on a white horse or in a chariot of fire and hurls thunderbolts at kulshedras. Because of this, he is identified in some regions with the mythological dragon. Elias is not only a Christian saint but also a weather god, he protected against storms and fires. Saint Elias took the place of the ancient sun god Helios. He is sometimes considered a reflection of Mithras's early sun cult. Christians used to venerate Saint Elias at the Bektashi tekke of Sersem Ali in Tetovo. In central Albania, the saint has been identified with Abbas Ali since the latter Muslim holy man lies buried high on Mount Tomor. Thus there is a lexical interference between the words Ali and Li. Saint Elias' feast day is July 20 when, in Albanian popular tradition, animals were sacrificed...."

Titus Livy in the book History of Rome, Vol III describes the campaign of the Roman army against the Macedonian army in the year 200 BC:

"...The consul, Sulpicius, who was at that time encamped; on the river Apsus, between Apollonia and Dyrrachium, having ordered Lucius Apustius, lieutenant-general, thither, sent him with part of the forces to lay waste the enemy's territory. Apustius, after ravaging the frontiers of Macedonia, and having, at the first assault, taking the forts of Corragos, Gerrunios, and Orgessos, came to Antipatria, a city situated in a narrow gorge; where, at first inviting the leading men to a conference, he endeavored to entice them to commit themselves to the good faith of the Romans, but finding that from confidence in the size, fortifications, and situation of their city, they paid no regard to his discourse; he attacked the place by force of arms, and took it by assault: then, putting all the young men to death,

---

[17] (see. Balkanistica13 (2000), pp. 35-57 or
His article "The Christian Saints of Albania")

and giving up the entire spoil to his soldiers, he razed the walls and burned the city. This proceeding spread such terror that condition, a strong and well-fortified town, surrendered to the Romans without a struggle. Leaving a garrison there, he took Ilion by force, a name is better known than the town on account of that of the same name in Asia "

Map; Ancient Macedonia, Thracia, Illyria, Moesia, and Dacia. They are published under the superintendence of the Society for the Diffusion of Useful Knowledge. J. & C. Walker Sculpt. Published March 1st. 1830 by Baldwin & Cradock, 47 Paternoster Row, London. (London: Chapman & Hall, 1844) Publication Author: Society for the Diffusion of Useful Knowledge (Great Britain)Collection: Rumsey Collection.2)Book; Titus Livy, book History of Rome, Vol IIIia...."

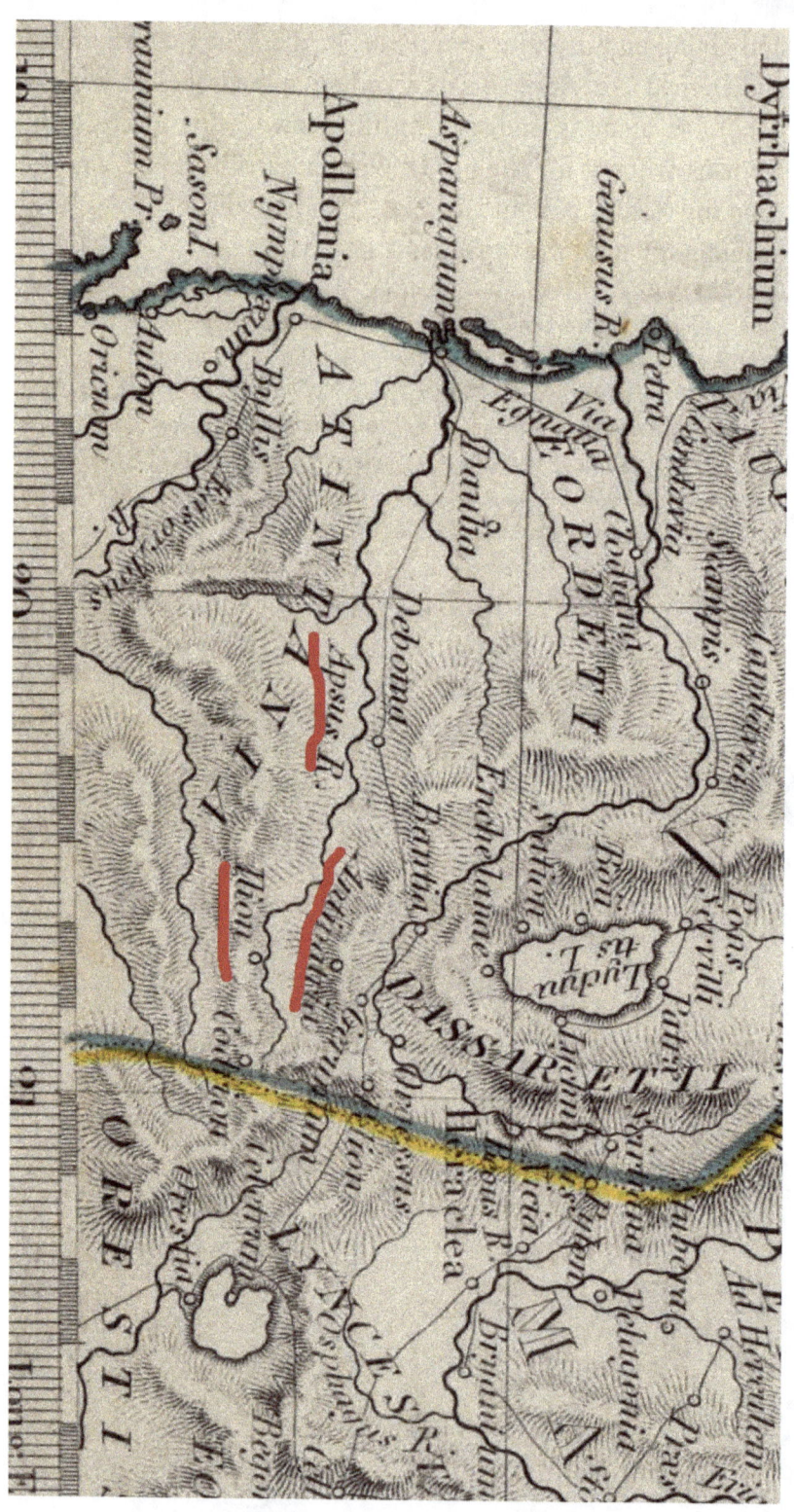

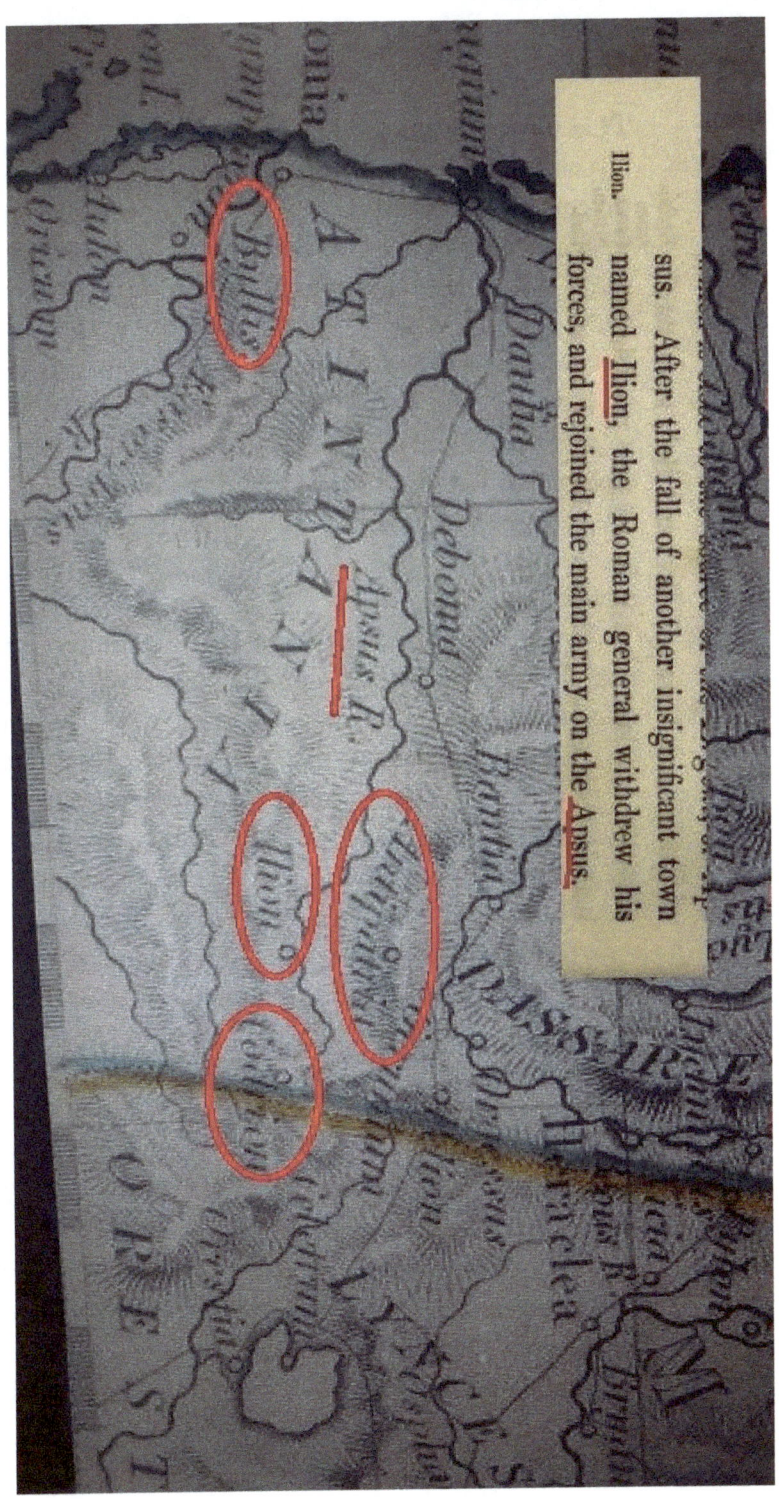

sus. After the fall of another insignificant town named Ilion, the Roman general withdrew his forces, and rejoined the main army on the Apsus.

Ilion.

This however was also stormed and destroyed. The fortress of Codrion surrendered. This place seems to correspond with the *Codras* in modern maps, which is close to the source of the *Ergent*, or Apsus. After the fall of another insignificant town named Ilion, the Roman general withdrew his forces, and rejoined the main army on the Apsus.

Codrion.

Ilion.

The Caliceni were another small tribe of Dassaretia noticed only by Polybius, (loc. cit.) their principal town was Bantia. Creonium is also named by the same writer among the Dassaretian towns taken by Philip. (loc. cit.) The whole of this district is now called *Caulonias*[1].

Caliceni.

Bantia. Creonium.

On the Macedonian border, and commanding the pass leading into that country, was Pelion, a place of considerable importance from its situation, and of which Arrian speaks at some length in his relation of an attack made upon it by Alexander in a war with the two Illyrian kings, Clitus and Glaucias. According to this historian it was surrounded by mountains, and close to a very narrow defile, through which flowed the river Eordaicus. On the defeat of the Illyrians it was abandoned by them and set on fire, (Exped. Alex. I. p. 5. et seq.) Arrian does not state that Pelion belonged to the Dassaretii; but this information we derive from Livy, who reports that it was taken by the consul Sulpicius in the first campaign against Philip. (XXXI. 40.) That officer was then returning from a successful irruption into Macedonia, during which he had traversed and laid waste several districts, especially Pelagonia, Eordæa, Elimea, and Orestis. It was from the latter point that he diverged into the country of the

Pelion.

[1] Pouqueville, t. I. p. 237.

Another book that identifies the Ilion city, which is located in the river Apsus (Today Osum), near Mount Tomor, and near Codrion city (Solve) is the book "A Geographical and Historical Description of Ancient Greece" With a Map, and a Plan of Athens, By John Anthony Cramer · 1828, p. 76.

Another author who is called John Wilkes, wrote :

"...After the Liburni, there come the Illyrian people. The Illyrii dwell by the sea as far as Chaonia, which lies opposite Corcyra, the island Alcinous. There is situated the Greek city called Heraclea, with a harbor. There dwell the Lotus-eaters and barbarian peoples with the names Hierastamnae, Bulini, and Hylli, who are neighbors of the Bulini. These people say that Hyllus, the son of Hercules, had his dwelling among them. They are a barbarian people occupying a peninsula a little smaller than the Peloponnese. The Bulini are also Illyrian people...." [18]

---

[18] (See John Wilkes "ILLYRI", page. 95, First Published USA 1992)
The original page of the book The original page of the book "ILLYRI", page. 95, John Wilkes, First Published USA 1992,

20 After the Veneti the river Ister. This river flows also into the Pontus Euxinus, facing in the direction of Egypt. The coastal voyage along the Istrian region lasts a day and a night.
21 After the Istri is the people of the Liburni. In the territory of that people are the following coastal cities: Lias, Idassa, Attienites, Dyyrta, Ampsi, Osi, Pedetae, Hemioni | - Alos, Tarsatica, Senites, Dyyrta, Lopsi, Ortopeletae, Hegini|. These people are ruled by women, who are the wives of freeborn men, but they cohabit with their own slaves and with the men of the neighbouring regions. Before the coast lie islands, of which I can record the following names (for there are many others which have no name): the island Istris 310 stades long and 120 stades wide, the Elektrides, and the Mentorides are the large islands. Then comes the (river) Catarbates. The voyage along the coast of the Liburni lasts two days.
22 After the Liburni there come the Illyrian people. The Illyrii dwell by the sea as far as Chaonia, which lies opposite Corcyra, the island of Alcinous. There is situated the Greek city called Heraclea, with a harbour. There dwell the Lotus-eaters, barbarian peoples with the names Hierastamnae, Bulini, and Hylli who are neighbours of the Bulini. This people tell that Hyllus the son of Hercules had his dwelling among them. They are a barbarian people occupying a peninsula a little smaller than the Peloponnese. The Bulini are also an Illyrian people. The voyage along the land of the Bulini as far as the river Nestus takes one day.

In this description John Wilkes among others, said that:

Hylli was neighboring the Byline tribe who were located in the area now called Malakastra.

But another author, Martin William Leak, who visited the Tomor area at the beginning of the century XIX, identified the city of Ilion (or Ilium). He has written in his book that:

"... Codrion and Ilium seem to have been in the valley of Uzumi above Berat on the slope of Tomor...."

> of the three. *Codrion* and *Ilium* seem to have been in the valley of the Uzúmi above Berát on the slopes of Tomór. This great mountain still bears probably its ancient name, of which the Greek form was *Tómarus*. It is easy to conceive that, like the names of mountains and rivers in general, Tomór was a generic word belonging to

"Travels in Northern Greece" Vol III, William Martin Leak, Page 328, Year 1835, Publisher J. Rodwell.

In the article" I POPOLI ED I CENTER ILLIRICI DELL'ANTICA ALBANIA" by Pellegrino C. Sestieri, is written:[19]

"...In the passage of Livy already cited (XXXI 27), we read that Apustio conquered Ilion, specifying that it is not the much better known and homonymous city in Asia Minor. However, in some manuscripts, Cnidus is read instead of Ilium, which is also a name of a city in Asia Minor. The Kiepert (Forma Orbis antiqui XVI) - (my note; Heinrich Kiepert was a German geographer and cartographer) accepts this last lesson, that of Cnidus, and then places this city near the Bregu Valasit, which is a hill that detaches itself from the southwestern slopes of Tomorri...."

---

[19] Published In: Iliria, vol. 4, 1976. Premier colloque des Etudes Illyriennes. (Tirana 15-20 septembre 1972) – 1. pp. 381-384,

Map; Image from; An atlas of ancient geography, biblical & classical: to illustrate the Dictionary of the Bible and the classical dictionaries / edited by William Smith and George Grove.Publication 1874.

According to my research, this place maybe is in the village of Vala. This village is located on the top of a hill. At the end of which, the two rivers meet. Osumi (Ancient Apsus) and Black Water. The hill where the village is located is separated from Tomori by the Osumi River.

Vala Village. Photo hy Besim Dervishi. Albania 2021.

But this city may have been in the Sulova area. In the place called "Imraj Castle" mentioned by Poliby. An Illyrian castle 982 m above sea level…." The most interesting fact is that during archeological excavations in the place called "Imraj Castle" in the North of Tomor Mountain, in the 1960s Archaeologists Frano Prendi and Dhimosten Budina discovered several ancient stamps, one of which read TPITOY TEXNA. Archaeologists also found other names like PATO, but the name TPITOY is important (this name was pronounced TRITU because in antiquity, the letter P was pronounced R, and the letters OY were pronounced U.

(Photo of Article: Kalaja e Irmajt (Germime te Vitit 1960) Frano Prendi, Dhimosten Budina, Iliria, Year 1972, Nr. 2, pp 21-60)

Part of a thematic issue : Qyteti Ilir. Botim i veçantë me rastin e «Kuvendit të parë të studimeve Ilire» mbajtur në Tiranë me

15-21 shtator 1972.

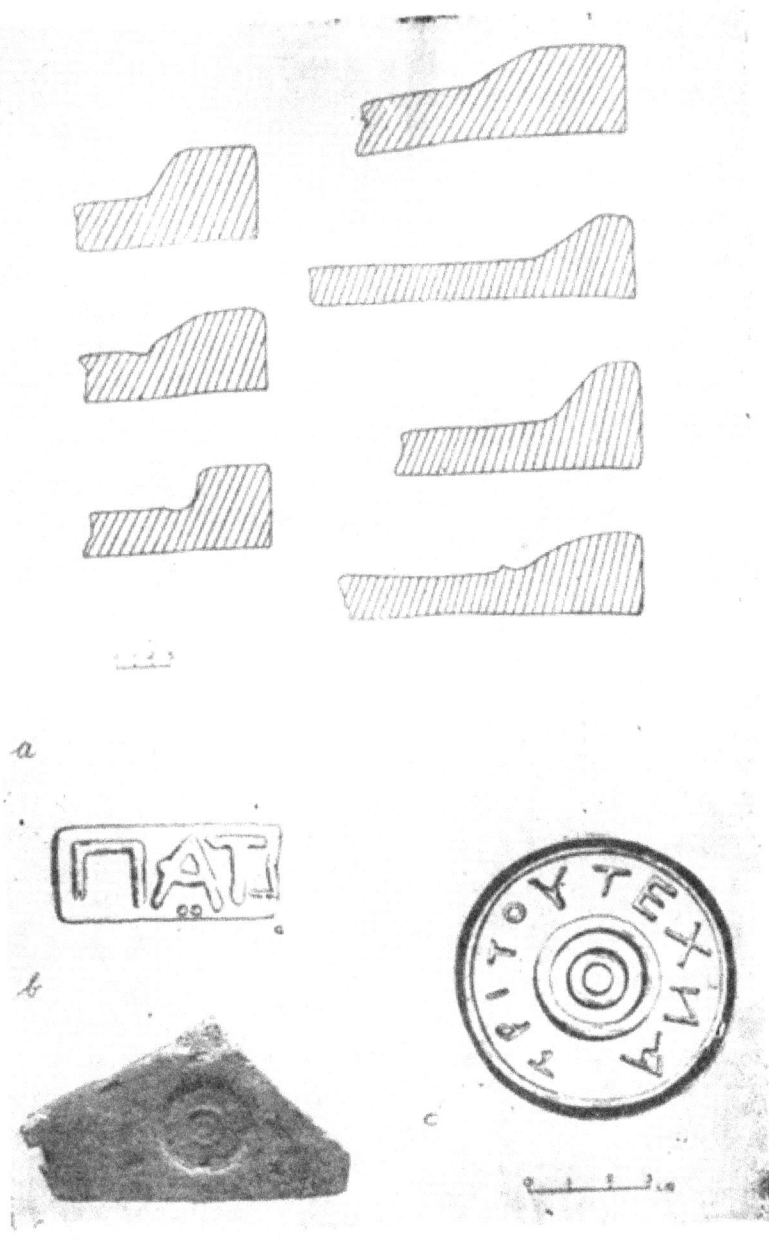

Tab. VIII

Photo of Article: Kalaja e Irmajt (Germime te Vitit 1960) Frano Prendi, Dhimosten Budina, Iliria, Year 1972, Nr. 2, pp 21-60. Tab VIII. On page 33 of Iliria magazine, the authors have said that the name TRIT was the Illyrian name, but without specifying its meaning.

According to historian Altin Kocaqi:

"...The city of Knossos in Crete, which is known as the oldest city in Europe, was called trita. This name is similar to tris, tria , dris, ndris, drita, (light in the Albanian Language). "Troins tis Ilion". Tris- Ilion= Sun=Dielli(in alb.). It is known from Homer as the old name of Troja, Ilion (in alb. Ylli). Facts are not just Homer's data in the "Iliad" but also the name Iliad, which was otherwise called Ilia, Yllja (the Star). "Troes," inhabitants of the city Ilion. The similarity of the name Tris, Troy in relation to the old name "Ilion" (Star), "Star" goes to "Light"..."[20]

Although on page 33 of their article in Iliria magazine, Frano Prendi and Dhimosten Budina thought that the words TRITOS, TRITOY....may be Illyrian names. I think the name TITRA, TRITOU, TRITIS, is the name of the city (Ilion). Or the name of Mount Tomor. Roman geography Vibius Sequester has identified Tomor with a similar name, "TENITRUS" (TENI- TRUS)

The exact identification of Tomor Mountain for the first time after the ancient author made Strabo of the IV century e.s. Vibius Sequester in the book entitled "De fluminibus, fontibus, lacubus, nemoribus, paludibus". On page 33 of this book, it is stated that "Tenitrus Macedonia, Proximus Apolloniae, in confpeftu Dyrrachii." (Mount Tenitrus (Tomarus) of Macedonia near Apollonia from where Dyrrahu is seen). The Roman author Vibius Sequester has made a book in which he accurately identifies the rivers, mountains, and lakes of the provinces in the Roman Empire.

20

(See; Altin Kocaqi in his book " Vendi i Shqipes Nder Gjuhet Evropiane" Tirane 2013, page 143)

> *Stefiarus Molofſiae. (*q*)
> Tarpejus Romae, ex VII. unus.
> Taenarus Laconices.
> Tmolus Lydiae, vino infignis. (*r*)
> Taburnus Samnitum, olivifer. (*s*)
> Taygeta Laconices. (*t*)
> Tericus Sabinorum. (*u*)
> *Tenitrus Macedoniae, proximus Apollo-
> niae, in confpectu Dyrrachii. (*x*)
> *Velinus Romae, ex VII. unus.
> Vefulus Apuliae.   *forfan* Liguriae.

1 – Page 33 of the book; De fluminibus, fontibus, lacubus, nemoribus, paludibus – Vibius Sequester

Tomor Mountain viewed from Durres (ancient Dyrrah) and Adriatic Sea. Photo by Tomorr Laze: December 17; 2021.

According to British author A. B. Cook; The Etruscan name for Zeus was —tin, tins, tinia: Zeus, god of the dark sky (earthquake, clouds, wind, dew, rain, meteorits): — Cambridge, 1940).[21] Tinia was the god of the sky, or Zeus to the Pelasgian people or Jupiter (Saturni) to the Roman. This name is similar to the name given to us by the roman author Sequester.

According to Manly Palmer Hall;

"....The Sun, A Universal Deity. The adoration of the sun was one of the earliest and most natural forms of religious expression. Complex modern theologies are merely involvements and amplifications of this simple aboriginal belief. The primitive mind, recognizing the beneficent power of the solar orb, adored it as the proxy of the Supreme Deity..."[22]

---

[21] (See A.B.Cook. Page 1113 in his book "Zeus: a study in ancient religion (Band 3,2): Zeus god of the dark sky (earthquake, clouds, wind, dew, rain, meteorits): — Cambridge, 1940).

One page further, on 135-136 of "The Solar Trinity", Hall said:

"...The sun, as supreme among the celestial bodies visible to the astronomers of antiquity, was assigned to the highest of the gods and became symbolic of the supreme authority of the Creator Himself. From a deep philosophic consideration of the powers and principles of the sun has come the concept of the Trinity as it is understood in the world today. The tenet of a Triune Divinity is not peculiar to Christian or Mosaic theology but forms a conspicuous part of the dogma of the greatest religions of both ancient and modern times. The Persians, Hindus, Babylonians, and Egyptians had their Trinities. In every instance, these represented the threefold form of one Supreme Intelligence."

The origin of the Trinity is evident to anyone who will observe the daily manifestations of the sun. This orb, being the symbol of all Light, has three distinct phases: rising, midday, and setting. The philosophers, therefore, divided the life of all things into three distinct parts: growth, maturity, and decay. Between the twilight of dawn and the twilight of the evening is the high noon of shining glory. God the Father, the Creator of the world, is symbolized by the dawn. His color is blue because the sun rising in the morning is veiled in blue mist. God the Son he Illuminating One sent to bear witness of His Father before all the worlds are the celestial globe at noonday, radiant and magnificent, the maned Lion of Judah, the Golden-haired Savior of the World. Yellow is His color, and His power is without end. God, the Holy Ghost, is the sunset phase, when the orb of day, robed in flaming red, rests for a moment upon

---

[22] (See book; Secret Teachings of All Ages Manly Palmer Hall, Chapter IX "The Sun a Universal Deity", page 134, USA 2003)

the horizon line and then vanishes into the darkness of the night to wander the lower worlds and later rise again triumphant from the embrace of darkness...."

According to Baba Ali Tomorri and Robert Elsie; bektashi in our area has come at the end of the century XIX, but in the year 1600:

"...In 1600 AD, Hadji Baba (Qesaraka) from the tekke of Hacibektas arrived at the top of Mount Tomor, and on that peak venerated by the Albanians since ancient times, he set a sign and told the people that the site would thereafter be visited in the name of Abbas Ali, the brother of Imam Husein and standard -bearer of Kerebela. After leaving this sign on Tomor, Hadji Baba went to Permeti, where he died. From there, his body was taken to Qesaraka in the Kolonja region, where a tekke and a tyrbe were built in his honor which still exist in all their glory to the present day. For three hundred years, BABA TOMOR, A MOUNTAIN OF THE PAGANS for two thousand years, has been a center of reverence for the great martyr of Kerebela and a true site of pilgrimage, being visited by all the Bektashi of Albania every year on August 12 [old style]..."

(Excerpt from "Ali Tomorri, Historia e Bektashinjeve[Tirane 1929] pp 82-94 Translated from Albanian by Robert Elsie. An Excerpt from Robert Elsie, The Albanian Bektashi History and Culture of a Dervish Order in the Balkan [Great Britain 2019 p. 81)

The truth is that in Tomor, there is no tomb of Abaz Ali, no arm was taken from his tomb, but a "Dervish" brought a fist soil the tomb of Abaz Ali and was thrown to the top of this mountain. While Tomor, was the center of the Pelasgian-Illyrian peoples. After her on this mountain was erected the church of the "Sun" and after the church the Bektashi shrine.

But we have another version that is older than the version of "Abbas Ali", published in his article, General Salle. In this article with the title "The Customs and Legends of Albania" from Revue Bleue, December 3, the year 1922, published in the book "The Living Age," Eight Series, Volume XXVI, Boston "The Living Age Company" the year 1922, p.44, p.45;

> The older Christians often wear a kind of white cloth bound about their hair. Among the peculiarities of costume — that of men as well as of women — it is to be noted that the fundamental colors of a costume and the embroideries are always the same. They are black with red embroidery, or red with black embroidery. The white color has appeared only in comparatively recent times, and only in the costumes of men. All the fabrics for their clothing are woven in the country itself.
>
> In the very centre of Albania towers a great mountain, reaching a height of more than two thousand feet and covered with snow for the greater part of the year, which the Albanians call Tomor. A belief widely spread among the Albanians has it that Tomor holds in its flanks the tomb of Jupiter, — although no one can quite establish the exact place of the tomb, — and at cer-

Page 44 of the book "The Living Age"

"...In the very center of Albania towers a great mountain, reaching a height of more than two thousand feet and covered with snow for the greater part of the year, which the Albanians call Tomor. A belief widely spread among the Albanians is that Tomor holds the tomb of Jupiter on its flanks — although no one can quite establish the exact place of the burial — and at certain times of the year, Jupiter brandishes his thunderbolts and makes the mountain resound with his imprecations. The oath, Per Baba Tomor (By Father Tomor), is customary among Christians and Mussulmans alike; and Baba Tomor, the holy mountain of the Albanians are as much honored in their country as was Olympus......"

> **THE BOOK OF WAN-HU-CHEN**
>
> tain times of the year Jupiter brandishes his thunderbolts and makes the mountain resound with his imprecations. The oath, *Per Baba Tomor* (By Father Tomor), is customary among Christians and Mussulmans alike; and Baba Tomor, the holy mountain of the Albanians, is as much honored in their country as was Olympus, dwelling-place of the king of the gods, among the ancient Greeks.
>
> One of the numerous Mussulman sects, known as the Bectachlis, counts numerous adherents in Albania. The Bectachlis are connected with the Tekkes monasteries, which are frequent in the country and are inhabited by dervishes living under the authority of a number of *babas*, or fathers superior. The Bectachlis' ranks are filled largely from rich Mohammedans who have the rank of bey, a title of nobility similar to that of count or baron. They believe in metempsychosis, profess the highest respect and devotion for the babas, fear their maledictions, and seek their benedictions. With this purpose in mind, many Bectachlis present the Tekkes with fields, mines, animals, even sums of money, so almost all these monasteries are rich and own numerous lands and freeholds.
>
> In the month of March the Bectachlis celebrate the birth of Ali, the cousin and son-in-law of Mahomet, whom they reverence even more than Mahomet himself. They have a Ramadan (month of fasting) of their own, during which they observe a strict fast from the rising to the setting of the sun, and abstain from taking any drink. This fast lasts for twelve days.

Page 45 of the book "The Living Age"

65

THE CIRCULAR STRUCTURE OF STONES AT THE NORTHERN TOP OF TOMOR

Photo published by Gazmend Shehu and friends.

(The circular structure could have been used as energy generating devices). According to the physical education teacher and athlete Mr. Gazmend Shehu:

The diameter of the "room" (Circular Structure of Stones) is about 5 m or 16.4 feet, the height from the inside is about 80 cm or 0.8 m (2.6 feet), while from the outside it goes to 110 cm, or 1.1 m (3.6 feet) because it is conical in shape. About two months ago, I had just gone there with three friends from Elbasan. They are living in the USA; I was eating something. Meanwhile, my wife got me on the phone, and I

communicated, but only at one point on the south side of the inner wall.

Photo published by Artur Guni

The road there passes through Qafe Dardha, from the Tariko Fountain, but this does not exclude other possibilities, but it takes longer. 1.5 months ago, I crossed again for the third time the ridge, from the south, from the tomb of Abaz Ali to the north, the peak we are talking about, ie, the highest peak, 2416m.

According to Mr. Gazmend Shehu, another way to go to the circular and stone structure is:

1) Tomor village - Stradom - Circular structure of stones or Lybesh- Peljes Neck- Circular Structure of the Stones.

Photo by Gazmend Shehu. Inside the circular structure of the stones

According to Durim Hazizi from the village of Tomor, during an interview with journalist Alma Cupi:

"He had heard from his father and his grandfather that in the northern part of Mount Tomor, there is a circular structure of stones. It was known as "Cuka of Mekamit" the "Cuka of Baba Tomori". Precisely in that place created a large flame of fire and discharged into the sea. But no one could explain this phenomenon."[23]

---

[23] (You can watch the show: "Histori shqiptare nga Alma Çupi - Shtegu i panjohur i malit te Tomorit" (17 shkurt 2018). Minutes from 18:40 - 19:00, TV KLAN. Or you can watch in this link
https://www.youtube.com/watch?v=SlY1xVnBBmM&t=1157s)

Tomor, August 2021 Photo by Besim Dervishi.

This photo was placed on the wall of the Bektashi Tekke on Tomori Mountain. They consider the circle of stones north of Mount Tomor as another Tomb of Abbas Ali. In fact, the stone circle was considered an orthodox shrine before the Bektashis, and before them was a pagan oracle. But there is evidence that The circular structure could have been used as an energy-generating device. We will talk about this below.

(Again, the circular structure could have been used as energy generating devices)[24]

Cook in the explanation that made this photo, says on page 67; fig. 913 the chapel of St. Elias from the southwest. According to Cook in this book(page 63). Zeus Superseded by Saint Elias.

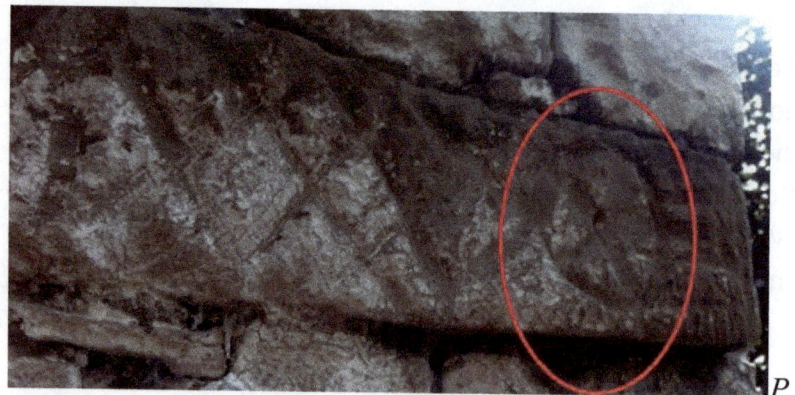

hoto by Krenar Kajo. First published by Besim Dervishi. A sacred stone was found in the village of Perisnaka, Berat. In the northern part of Mount Tomor.

---

[24]) Photo by Colonel D. R. Oakley Hill. First published by Arthur Bernard Cook in his book "Zeus A Study in Ancient Religion · Volume 3, Part 2" page 70. Under 1940.

Perikli Ikonomi, in the book "History of Tomor. The Pelasgian Dodona and Tomor God of the Pelasgians," on page 26 tells a story that:

"... Fever when a patient leaves, the women say that Tomori took it, that the fever went away and they went to Tomor, so Tomori took it ..."

This is true. In ancient times, the sites of oracles that were discovered in Africa today by Michael Tellinger and other archaeologists (who appear in the form of a circular stone structure) were places where some diseases were cured. National Geographic photographer and anthropologist Martin Gray has spent thirty-five years studying and photographing 1500 of these sacred sites in more than one hundred and sixty countries.

Here is what he says:

"...Since ancient times, certain places have had a powerful attraction for billions of people around the world. Known as sacred sites and pilgrimage places, they are the most venerated and iconic locations of human civilization. Legends and contemporary reports tell of extraordinary experiences people have had while visiting these holy places. Different sacred sites have the power to heal the body, enlighten the mind and inspire the heart...."[25]

This particular stone represents the sketch of what can be called an antique "battery".

According to the author of the books "Mysteries of the Ancient Past", "Lost Knowledge of the Ancients", and "Spirits

---

[25] (Reference "The Power of Place: Sacred Sites and the Presence of the Miraculous, Martin Gray, June 17, 202. Web: https://www.youtube.com/watch?v=IMHTlOJrzX0&t=66s)

in Stone,". Glenn Kreisberg, which also is Radio Frequency (RF) Spectrum Engineer, outdoor guide, and radio engineer, who researches archaeoastronomy and landscape archaeology, says that:

".... It's been suggested, at various times, that ancient humans had the knowledge and use of unseen powers, forces, and energy fields(My note; as the force of the wind, the sound).

For the vanished civilizations and cultures of Egypt, Sumer, and other early civilizations, and actually for the entire lapsed time of humankind, there remain many unsolved and unsettling images, messages, texts, tablets, artifacts, inscriptions, engravings, schemes, and phenomena that suggest a connection to unseen forces. Most significant, for this report, are the many variations of the basic waveforms, a saw-tooth wave, box wave, or the endless variety of spirals and waveforms that adorn ancient cave walls, temples, and structures and appear in architecture, scrolls, tablets, and inscriptions throughout the ancient world..."

Below is his article entitled "Did Ancient Humans Have Knowledge of the Electromagnetic (EM) Spectrum?"[26]

He gives us some examples of waveform symbols appearing in ancient designs and motifs that existed in ancient cultures from around the world. In China, La Pirámide de Chichen Itza (Temple of Kukulcán) Mexico), Temple of Mnajdra on Malta.In the stone that was found in the village of Perisnak Tomor. An image is engraved on the surface of the stone. The stone structures found in these places are sawtooth waves. Zigzag waves in the tooth form gather at the entrance of a circle. Waves (which can be frequencies or sounds caused by the wind) enter inside it. Inside the circle are found two lines

---

[26] By Glenn Kreisberg. Author links:overlookmountain.org
Published 21st November 2005, but also in his books.

that intersect. The place where they intersect is the center of the circle, and it is marked with a point that symbolizes "the navel of the world" or "the center of the world." The inhabitants of the area still believe a legend that Tomori is the navel of the world" and "the center of the world." And if it opens, the world will be flooded. This legend reminds you of the great flood.

After waves or sounds enter the circle, an electromagnetic field is created. Outside the process are some lines, which symbolize energy that benefited from waves and sounds. According to Wassa Pasha and Sir P. Colquhoun. Published in the boo, "THE ASIATIC QUARTERLY REVIEW".NEW SERIES - VOLUME III .JANUARY - APRIL, 1892.LONDON, (p. 211 and p.212). Published in their article, "The Pelasgi and their Modern Descendants," it is written that:

Strabo says Troy was built on a low hill, λόφος οὐκ ὑψιλὸς.

Now it is a recognised fact, that the Pelasgi, or some tribes of them, were driven by others from the neighbourhood of the sea shore, and, emigrating with their deities towards the hills, found a more secure retreat. Thus the frequent sites represent only the various stages which the Pelasgian Ze made in his various migrations.

In describing this site of the ancient Dodona, the Pelasgian Ze is described as dwelling on the heights of Mount Tomaros, defying the winds and the ice, and thence sending forth his thunders. The object, then, is to discover this Mount Tomaros. One actually exists in the Molopide and Theoprotia, near to the town of Berat; to seek for it in the lowlands of Arta is therefore absurd. Within a few hours of Berat there is a mountain called by the natives, "Tomor," in the plain at the foot of which lie some scattered villages inhabited by Mussulman Albanians. On the summit of this mountain may be seen a number of stunted oaks. The path leading to it is extremely precipitous, and frequented only by goats and chamois. The natives have a superstition, that the summit of this mountain cannot be reached with impunity; that he would be impious who attempted it, and would not return alive; and that some mysterious power resides there which they call I-mir-i-Tomorit, the good genius of Tomor. I-mir, or the Good, is equivalent to the god. Strange noises, probably the effect of atmospheric influences, are from time to time heard on the summit; these in ancient times were held to be the voice of the god. According to the intensity of these sounds, the surrounding peasants draw prognostications of a good or bad harvest, epidemics, wars, and the like; and when at a distance from their native land, affirm Per-i-mir i Tomor, Per Zee-i-Tomorit i-Ζευς; and this, notwithstanding the change of religion, has been handed down among the people. This raises a strong presumption that Mount Tomor was the last station of the Pelasgic Ze, in his repeated migrations towards the more inaccessible country, under the pressure of some Pelasgic or other tribes from posi-

"...Now it is a recognized fact that the Pelasgi, or some of their tribes, were driven out by others from their locations near the sea shore and, emigrating with their deities towards the hills, found a more secure retreat. Thus the frequent sites represent only the various stages that the Pelasgian Ze made in their various migrations."

In describing this site of the ancient Dodona, the Pelasgian Ze is described as dwelling on the heights of Mount Tomaros, defying the winds and the ice, and thence sending forth his thunders. The objective, then, is to discover Mount Tomaros. It actually exists in the Molopide and Thesprotia, near Berat's town; seeking it in Arta's low lands is absurd. Within a few hours of Berat there is a mountain called by the natives, "Tomor," in the plain at the foot of which lie some scattered villages inhabited by Mussulman Albanians.

A number of stunted oaks may be on the summit of this mountain. The path leading to it is exceptionally precipitous and frequented only by goats and chamois. The natives have a superstition that the summit of this mountain cannot be reached with impunity; that he would be impious who attempted it, and would not return alive; and that some mysterious power resides there which they call i - mir - i - Tomorit , the good genius of Tomor . I- mir , or the Good, is equivalent to God. Strange noises, probably the effect of atmospheric influences, are from time to time heard on the summit; these in ancient times were held to be the voice of God. According to the intensity of these sounds, the surrounding peasants draw prognostics of a good or bad harvest, epidemics, wars, and the like; and when at a distance from their native land, affirm Per - i - mir i Tomor, Per Zee - i - Tomorit i - Zeus; and this, notwithstanding the change of religion, has been handed down among the people. This raises a strong presumption that Mount Tomor was the last station of the Pelasgic Ze, in his repeated migrations towards the more inaccessible country, under the pressure of some

Pelasgic or other tribes from positions nearer the sea - shore...."

According to researcher, Perikli Ikonomi published in his book, "History of Tomori. Dodona Pelasgian and Tomor God of the Pelasgians" p 22.

"...On the Mount Tomor there is a wind or air current which is called "Stocen". According to him, this word resembles the word "Stercenius" (Latin word). Which is the name of an old god..."

This air current is very strong, especially at the top, where is the circular structure of the stone. The northern peak is the stones' circular structure (2416m). It has various names. One is "The Peak of the Voice" (Cuka e Zes). The inhabitants confuse it with the word "Ze" (voice, sound). This Albanian word resembles the Albanian word "Zezë (which means black).

According to the book "THE TRUTH ABOUT ALBANIA AND ALBANIANS," "PAGE 12 ... the YEAR 1887, PASHKO VASA, PUBLISHED IN GERMANY, TRANSLATED BY SKENDER MACI (2000), it is written:

"...By Reha was born Zeus; Zâ; Zë, in Albanian means: voice. Reha could not be born except through the spark, the explosion, the explosion which gave a tone. This is thunder and lightning, precisely the voice (Zaani, Zeeri) of the Pelasgians. We know that Zeus, his Dodonian Oracle, made noise through a voice, and therefore, Zeer, Zee, was the lord of the Pelasgians. This word Zaa, Zee was later transformed into Zaan, Zoon, Zoot, and today God, which means god and people swear by Zoon, Zoot, God..." (see p. 12).

In conclusion, the circular structure of the stone is located on the northern top of Tomor, where air currents circulate as the wind, known by the name "Stoceni". In ancient times it was a pagan temple. Scheme of operation of this temple It is carved on the stone found in the village of Perisnak, which is located 2-3 km away from the northern top of the mountain. Voice, sound, wind, and water have been used across oracles as energy sources. The circular stone structure has been identified in the world through other oracles in America, Europe (Malta), Africa, and Asia.

The power of sound, voice, wind, and wave will not be underestimated. Waves and sound today are the basis, do not forget the sound waves, wires, and telephone waves.

"...If you are going to discover the secrets of the universe, think about the phenomena of frequency, sound, energy, and vibration...." N. Tesla.

The strength and power of the "Stocen" wind.

The British author R. Mathews also tells us in one of his stories. Who visited the top of Tomor Mountain in the late 1930s.

Excerpts from the article "BABA TOMOR - THE HOLY PLACE OF ALBANIANS," "Sunday Times" newspaper page 9, December 15, 1940. Author Ronald Mathews.

"...At present, the pilgrimage is managed by Bektashi dervishes who say that the sacred spot on the top is the second grave of Abbas Ali, a Shia saint buried in Mesopotamia and adopted by the Bektashis. There is good evidence that the cult on Tomor is older than the Bektashis, who were not found till the 14th century of our era. The primitive beliefs about the sanctity of the mountain seem to survive from a mountain cult, similar to those practiced in Biblical times on Horeb and Sinai."

In 1931 the first foreigner to make the pilgrimage stood in glorious sunshine on the mountain top. Scores of pilgrims were busy with their sacrifices and devotions when a sudden squall struck the summit; a little more, and the wind might have *flung them over the precipice.*

"He is angry today." muttered a pilgrim.

"Who is HE? Asked a visitor.

"The mountain." said the pilgrim. "Father Tomor." Said a bolder spirit."

DODONA CITY

QYTETI(The City). Photo by Medi Canko. First published by Besim Dervishi.

In this chapter, I explore the spiritual foundations of Dodona City. First, I introduce my argument and defend it with artifacts to prove that the spiritual foundations of Dodona City are based on the common belief that the city was created as a sanctuary for the dwellers or other travelers who came to the area for spiritual growth. Of great interest in this chapter are the discussion of the orphic egg, a symbol of fertility, and the genesis of the Universe in a much more effeminized, pagan perception. Hence, this chapter will offer a few points of view about the creation and flourishing of Dodona City. The In 1940, the British historian A. B. Cook wrote:

"...If you go to Mount Tomori (Tomarus) in South Albania today, you will eventually reach a village itself called Tomori. Above it is a collection of ruins, so far unexplored and known locally as QYTETI (the city)....and named by the villagers DODONA. In describing this site of the ancient Dodona, the Pelasgian ZE (ZEUS) is described as dwelling on the heights of Moun Tomarus, defying the winds and the ice, and sending forth his thunders. The object, then, is to discover this mount Tomaros. One exists near to the old town of Berat in Albania...."[27]

> Addenda   1171
>
> the autumn, a windfall will roll down the rocks to the turf below. Peasants who pass at that time of year always look to see if there is one there, for those great apples, they say, have the power of healing all diseases. Even the dying, I have heard men say, can be brought back to life if such a fruit is given them." Mr Matthews ends his narrative by noting the resemblance between Tomori in the north and Tomaros in the south: *ib.* p. 286 'if you go one way up Tomori to-day, you will eventually reach a village, itself called Tomori. Above it is a collection of ruins, so far unexplored, and known locally as Qyteti (the city). And the biggest among them is named by the villagers Dodona.'

Page 1171, book "Zeus: A Study in Ancient Religion, Volume 3, Part 2.

By A. B. Cook. Page 1171. It was first published in 1940 in the USA by Cambridge University Press, New York. The same data was written by the British author Ronald Matthews in his book entitled "SONS OF THE EAGLE." On page 286 of this book, he says:

"...But you go one way up Tomori today, you will eventually reach a village, itself called Tomori. Above it is a collection of ruins, so far unexplored and known locally as QYTETI (the city). And named by the villagers DODONA."

(See; "SONS OF THE EAGLE" By Ronald Matthews. Page 286. It the first published in 1937 by Methuen &Co. Ltd., London. Printed in Great Britain)

> 286   SONS OF THE EAGLE
>
> But if you go one way up Tomori to-day, you will eventually reach a village, itself called Tomori. Above it is a collection of ruins, so far unexplored, and known locally as Qyteti (the city). And the biggest among them is named by the villagers Dodona.

---

[27] Page 1171, book " Zeus: A Study in Ancient Religion, Volume 3, Part 2 By A. B. Cook. Page 1171. The first published 1940, USA by Cambridge University Press, New York.

(Page 286 of Book "SONS OF THE EAGLE" By Ronald Matthews. It was first published in 1937 by Methuen &Co. Ltd., London,. Printed in Great Britain.)[28]

Matthew, who has been to Tomor, has written other details in the book. The Albanian historian Perikli Ikonomi in his study of :Tomor, this ancient city," says that:

"... The city, placed on the site of Tomor, from the West, is a very strong place and is likened to a castle of nature with large stones like crates. This place is located above the village of Tomor below the place (Maja e Matit), which is called "Cuka e Peljes" (Peljus is the name by which the oracle priests were called) and "Stradomi" (Saturn Domi or the house of Saturn). This kind of natural castle is probably the stronghold that Strabo mentions, saying:

Dodona is a strong place. The name "Qyteza" should be studied because the mention of the name "Qyteza" may indicate that Dodona is nearby "(see Perikli Ikonomi).

In his book entitled "The Greek Myths" with author Robert Graves, Published in New York, G. Braziller,1957, Volume One, Chapter "THE PELASGIAN CREATION MYTH", pages 27-28 said:

"...In the beginning, Eurynome, the Goddess of All Things, rose naked from chaos but found nothing substantial for her feet to rest upon, and therefore divided the sea from the sky, dancing lonely upon its waves. She danced towards the south, and the wind set in motion behind her seemed something new and apart with which to begin work of creation. Wheeling

---

[28] (See; "SONS OF THE EAGLE" By Ronald Matthews. Page 286. It the first published in 1937 by Methuen &Co. Ltd., London. Printed in Great Britain)

about, she caught hold of this north wind, rubbed it between her hands, and behold!

The great serpent Ophion. Eurynome danced to warm himself, wildly and more wildly, until Ophion, grown lustful, coiled about those divine limbs and was moved to couple with her. Now, the North Wind, which is also called Boreas, fertilizes, which is why mares often turn their hindquarters to the wind and breed foals without the aid of a stallion. "So Eurynome was likewise got with child. (See; Pliny : Natural History iv . 35 and viü. 67 ; Homer : Iliad xx . 223)

Orphic Egg. Graffit by Zaim Gode. The graffiti was made based on the graffiti of Jacob Bryant. Orphic Egg (1774)

B. Next, she assumed the form of a dove, brooding on the waves, and, in due process of time, laid the Universal Egg. At her bidding, Ophion coiled seven times about this egg until it hatched and split in two. Out tumbled all things that exist, her children: sun, moon, planets, stars, the earth with its mountains and rivers, its trees, herbs, and living creatures.

C. Eurynome and Ophion made their home upon Mount Olympus, where he vexed her by claiming to be the author of the Universe. Forthwith she bruised his head with her heel, kicked out his teeth, and banished him to the dark caves below the earth.[29]

D. Next, the Goddess created the seven planetary powers, setting a Titaness and a Titan over each. Theia and Hyperion for the Sun; Phoebe and Atlas for the Moon; Dione and Crius for the planet Mars; Metis and Coeus for the planet Mercury; Themis and Eurymedon for the planet Jupiter; Tethys and Oceanus for Venus; Rhea and Cronus for the planet Saturn.3 But the first man was Pelasgus, ancestor of the Pelasgians; he sprang from the soil of Arcadia, followed by certain others whom he taught to make huts and feed upon acorns and sew pig-skin tunics such poor folk still wear in Euboea and Phocis.

---

[29] (See: Only tantalizing fragments of this pre-Hellenic myth survive in Greek literature, the largest being Apollonius Rhodius's Argo Nautica i. 496 – sos and Tzetzes: On Lycophron 1191; but it is implicit in the Orphic Mysteries, and can be restored, as above, from the Berossian Fragment and the Phoenician cosmogonies quoted by Philo Byblius and Damascius; from the Canaanitish elements in the Hebrew Creation story; from Hyginus (Fabula 197 – see 62. a); from the Boeotian legend of the dragon's teeth (see 58. 5), and from early ritual art. That all Pelasgians were born from Ophion is suggested by their common sacrifice, the Peloria (Athenaeus xiv. 45. 639–40), Ophion having been a Pelor or prodigious serpent)

Mithras was born from the Cosmic Egg. Graffit by Zaim Gode. A copy of one of her artifacts is in the Hancock Museum, Newcastle upon Tyne, Tyne and Wear, UK. A foreign expedition had found two artifacts in the "City." Mithras and Cosmic Egg

The "Spiritual Archeology" page posted 2017 some photos from the searches of some foreign tourists who have visited Mount Tomor.

"...Spiritual Archeology is a new trend in archeology started by archeologist, researcher of ancient cultures, and spiritual pathfinder - Tomasz Lelewski. It connects the past with information, knowledge, insights, Wisdom, and messages from Spirits & Akashic records...."

This page is administered by Tomasz Lelewski, an archeologist, researcher of ancient cultures, and spiritual pathfinder. He studied at Warsaw University, Institute of Archeology from 2000 to 2003. The Polish archaeologist came to Albania with two other tourists, Andrei Miklic and Alžbeta Goljerova.

On October 12, 2017, the "Spiritual Archeology" page on the social network Facebook posted some photos in a place called "City ." The site is located near the village of Tomor, near Tomor Castle. In a picture where you can see the rock of Tomori Castle, it's a footnote;

"...Berat county: I was told by a National Park worker that it is called "Dodona Temple," I called it Elephant Temple. The visible ruined face of an elephant."

Photo by Archeologist/Researcher - Tomasz Lelewski. The "Spiritual Archeology" page on the social network Facebook on October 12, 2017.

To use the photos taken in the ancient city above the village of Tomor, I asked for permission from the author of the images and the administrator of the Spiritual Archeology page on the Facebook social network, the archaeologist and researcher - Tomasz Lelewski. He replied to my email address. He agreed to use his photos on the condition that we include his name; He wrote:[30]

Two other photos were published by the "Spiritual Archeology" page on the social network Facebook on October

---

[30] "...Dear Beso,
I want to apologize for the slight delay in answering your question. Pretty busy this time. :))
I agree to use my photos and discoveries in Albania for your book on the condition of using my full name and position. Please find below: Archeologist/Researcher - Tomasz Lelewski
I look forward to hearing from you soon and receiving a copy of your book. Thank you and good luck.
P.S. If you have any questions about my discoveries, please don't hesitate to contact me.
Kind regards
Tomasz Lelewski"

12, 2017. People who have been to a place called "City" near the village of Tomor have posted two artifacts found near the Castle and the ancient city. In a photo where you can see the ancient artifact, it's a footnote:

"Berat county: Around Elephant Temple Betka Goljerova found the perfectly egg-shaped stone."

In footnotes, there are two essential elements. This page (Spiritual Archeology) calls Tomor Castle the "Elephant Temple". Second on this page, we have the name of the person who found the artifact. Her name is Betka Goljerova. She is a foreign national from Slovakia. The artifact is a perfectly egg-shaped stone which is very similar to Orphic Egg.

Orphic Egg. Photo by Archeologist/Researcher - Tomasz Lelewski. Published by the "Spiritual Archeology" page on Facebook, October 12, 2017. Found by Betka Goljerova(Alžbeta Goljerova, Slovakia). It is found near a place called Tomor Castle.

Again, in the "Spiritual Archeology" page on the social network Facebook, October 12, 2017, an ancient stone artifact has been posted. In a photo where you can see the ancient artifact. It is in a footnote. "Berat county: Around Elephant Temple, I found the head of the sculpture. Visible Humanoid face with ear and hair or hat."

 Oct 12, 2017

#45. Berat county: Around Elephant Temple I found head of the sculpture. Visible Humanoid face with ear and hair or hat.

Photo by Archeologist/Researcher - Tomasz Lelewski. Published by the "Spiritual Archeology" page on the social network Facebook, October 12, 2017. It is found near a place called Tomor Castle.

There is no doubt that these artifacts are the "Cosmic Egg" and "Mithras". However, their location remains enigmatic. It would be helpful to inquire with the researchers who found the artifact and the page administrator of Spiritual Archeology because this artifact carries a significant importance and may be a strong proof of the Pelasgian antiquity of Mount Tomor.

Canadian-American author Manly Palmer Hall in his book with the title "Secret Teachings of All Ages" says:

"...Chief of the Orphic symbols was the mundane egg from which Phanes sprang into light. Thomas Taylor considers the Orphic egg to be synonymous with the mixture from infinity mentioned by Plato in the Philebus. The egg is furthermore, the third Intelligible Triad and the proper symbol of the Demiurgus, whose auric body is the egg of the inferior Universe. Eusebius, on the authority of Porphyry, declared that the Egyptians acknowledged one intellectual Author or Creator of the world under the name of Cneph. They worshiped him in a statue of human form and dark blue complexion, holding in his hand a girdle and a scepter, wearing on his head a royal plume, and thrusting forth an egg out of his mouth."[31]

While the Bembine Table is rectangular-shaped, it signifies philosophically the Orphic egg of the Universe with its contents. In the esoteric doctrines, the supreme individual achievement is the breaking of the Orphic egg, which is equivalent to the return of the spirit to the Nirvana--the absolute condition--of the Oriental mystics..."[32]

---

[31] See An Analysis of the Egyptian Mythology

[32] (See "Secret Teachings of All Ages" Manly Palmer Hall, Page 176 and

Tomasz Lelewski an archeologist, researcher of ancient cultures, spiritual pathfinder, administers the page Spiritual Archeology. Lelewsky, studied Archeology at the University of Warsaw Poland and has posted many other photos taken in Tomori Castle and the ancient city near it. Among others he says:

"...Berat county: Ruins of Temples, Shrines and other structures on side of the Elephant Temple."

Photo by Archeologist/Researcher - Tomasz Lelewski.
Published by the "Spiritual Archeology" page on the social media Facebook, October 12 2017.

In this photo, he calls Tomor Castle the Temple of the Elephant. Lelewsky believes that the ruins found on the side of the castle are shrines.

" Berat county: On the way to castle Tomor. Another "emergency" stop to find this in the middle of nowhere. Surface looks like designed sculptures."

177, USA 2003, . Original text published in 1928)

While I think these symbols on the surface of the stones, are symbols of an ancient map or the way to a holy place which is located nearby.

While the stone is on the way to the ancient city near the village of Tomor. It must have been an ancient symbol that indicated the way to this city.

In conclusion, I presented a panoramic view of Dodona City and its spiritual foundations. Then, I explained thoughts and various beliefs about the creation of the Universe and how those beliefs affected the building of Dodona City. Finally, to defend my hypothesis that Dodona was, in fact, not only a spiritual center of an ancient civilization but also a civic one, I presented evidence from other archeologists, such as the work of Lelewsky. I defended the argument that spiritual practices drove the development of the ancient city. The philosophical thoughts behind the practices relied on a particular rationale about the Universe – which we do not see in other ancient philosophies or religions. This particularity makes Dodona City unique and intriguing since it contradicts the overall idea of the genesis of the Universe stated in various scriptures. In the next chapter, I present more details that I was able to gather during my exploration of Mount Tomor and its sacred places.

CONCLUSION

Before I embarked on this journey, I asked myself a few questions that baffled me for many years. I was born in this historical area of Albania, a place filled with myths, legends, and various hypotheses – that perhaps are left unanswered. To me, it was not only personal but also a tribute to people who have been and are part of Mount Tomor for centuries to take a stance and show that Tomor is in fact a mystical mountain, filled with mysteries', legends and no one better than me can tell the story of many gods and goddesses that once were oracles. Thus, these questions were part of my rational to shed light on Mount Tomor.

Why did I decide to write this book? Why did I publish the artifacts, terracottas, ancient coins, ancient writings, and stone statues found around Mount Tomor? Why have I written some toponyms for places, villages, and areas around Mount Tomor? Why did I write about the history and legends that connect with this mountain? Why is Mount Tomor different from other mountains? Why was Mount Tomor and is a symbol of the Illyrian-Albanian people? Why was Mount Tomor the center of the Illyrian-Albanians, and what are some facts that connect the mountain with the place where the Oracle of Dodona was?

  I decided to write this book to use facts as a counterargument against claims made by various historians and archaeologists who argue that Tomor was not a part of antiquity, nor does it have an archeological value. The ancient city near the village of Tomor, the area of Sulove called the city Chrisondion or Codrion; cities and archaeological sites such as Selan, Dobrushë, Tomorricë, prove that this mountain was part of antiquity. Furthermore, the stone tools in the village of Vlushe (years 70-80) reveal the presence of settlements during the Mezoneolithic Period. Other pieces of evidence are the two sphinxes carved in stone (between the villages of Bargulas and Kapinova).

  The stone tools found inside the ancient ruins and near the sphinx show that this archaeological site is ancient. These stone tools, as well as artifacts carved in stone, tell us about an early period. However, we need a complete study by researchers in the field of archeology. Then, we can say that this ancient archaeological site must exist since the Paleolithic Era (or Old Stone Age) or The Neolithic Era (or New Stone Age). According to archaeologists, the first period (The Paleolithic Era (or Old Stone Age) goes from 2.5 million years to 10,000 years BC, while the second period, The Neolithic Era (or New Stone Age), starts from 10,000 and ends from 4000 to 2000 BC. Even the finding of Terracotta in the Tomorice area is strong proof of the millennial antiquity of this mountain. This terracotta resembles the "Goddess on the Throne" found in Kosovo and other places, which according to researchers, it belongs to the so-called Danubian Culture.

Archaeologists think that the so-called Danubian Culture has an age of 5500-6000 years before Christ, so the age of terracotta can be up to 8,000 years old. The Pelasgian character of Mount Tomor is proved by the findings of the Polish researcher and archaeologist Tomasz Lelewski, which is similar to the Orphic Egg. There are two artifacts that tell us about the Pelasgian Creation Myth. According to "The Greek Myths" with author Robert Graves, Published New York, G. Braziller, 1957, Volume One, Chapter "THE PELASGIAN CREATION MYTH," page 27-28;

"...Eurynome, the Goddess of All Things, assumed the form of a dove, brooding on the waves and laid the Universal Egg at the due process. At her bidding, Ophion coiled seven times about this egg until it hatched and split in two. Out tumbled all things that exist, her children: sun, moon, planets, stars, the earth with its mountains and rivers, its trees, herbs, and living creatures...." The Pelasgian character of the mountain is proven by the cyclopean or Pelasgian walls in the ancient city above the village of Tomor, the cyclopean walls of Sulova, the Pelasgian walls in the town of Bargullas, which often measure 3 meters by 4-5 meters. Cyclopean stones are still found in the fortress of "Fushe Peshtan." But such rocks are located in the foundations of Berat Castle close to the castle's entrance. *(Refer to the Three photographs of cyclopean stones in Berat Castle. Berat, June 2021, Photo by Besim Dervishi.)*

In the mysterious settlement that we discovered for the first time, between the villages of Bargullas and Kapinove, there are square-shaped stones of gigantic size, ranging from 3-4 meters wide. We have taken photos of some of these stones and published them in this book. Tomor Mount Mountain has a very ancient history and wants to be discovered from the darkness of centuries.

Based on artifacts and the literature I presented, I believe the mountain was the first civic center in Europe and beyond. As is known, the first civic center in Europe was the Oracle of Dodona. Still, today science and archeology recognize the old ruins near Ioannina as where this Oracle was. This is based on the discoveries of Constantine Carapanos, a diplomat and a lawyer.

But science today has determined that the artifacts discovered in Ioannina do not date back more than the 4th or 5th century BC. Meanwhile, only the stone sphinxes near the village of Bargullas can be thousands of years old. Also, the discovery of the Orphic Egg and the Mither Head by the Polish expedition with the archaeologist and researcher Tomasz Lelewski tells us clearly the antiquity of Mount Tomor and its Pelasgian character. Both artifacts are examples of Pelasgian mythology. Also, a coin and the body of an arrow found in the castle of Gradishte (Fushe Peshtan village) contain symbols and writings that tell us about the antiquity of Mount Tomor. For example, one of the coins that we presented is the writing "KI," which, according to researchers, is thought to be the Illyrian word "KY" which in English means "THIS" or "IT".

This volume and body of research will be followed by two more volumes to complete my study and hypotheses on Mount Tomor and its significance in the region, but also in various cultures.

ANNOTATED BIBLIOGRAPHY

1 - Ikonomi, P. (1936) History of Tomor. Pelasgian Dodona And Tomor God of the Pelasgians. Vlora Albania The printing press "Atdheu". Pp 1- 34

2- Edwin E. Jasques - "The Albanians: An Ethnic History from Prehistoric Times to the Present", page 398

3- Arthur Bernard Cook Zeus : a study in ancient religion, Publisher Cambridge, Publication 1940, page 7, 178, 179, 186,187,

4- ΡΙΚΑΚΗ Ε. "ΒΕΡΑΤΙΟΝ ΙΣΤΟΡΙΚΗ, ΑΡΧΑΙΟΛΟΓΙΚΗ ΚΑΙ ΛΑΟΓΡΑΦΙΚΗ ΠΡΑΓΜΑΤΕΙΑ ΤΟΥ ΤΜΗΜΑΤΟΣ ΒΕΡΑΤΙΟΥ" ("History, Archeology, and Folklore for Berat"), published; ΕΝ ΑΘΗΝΑΙΣ ΤΥΠΟΓΡΑΦΕΙΟΝ 'ΕΣΤΙΑ', Κ. ΜΑΪΣΝΕΡ ΚΑΙ Ν. ΚΑΡΓΑΔΟΥΡΗ 1910. P. 1, 2, 3 ,4, 5, 6, 7, 8, 9.

5- Agani F. "Voice of intelligence for the national cause"
published in Pristina Kosovo, 1995, page 94

6- Carapanos C. Dodone et ses ruines, Paris: Hachette, 1878

7- Mathews R. "SONS OF THE EAGLE", First published in 1937, Methuen & Co.Ltd., London, Pp 273 - 286, 284– 285

8- Kocaqi A., Article "Gjurmë pellazgjike në Tomor. Simboli i Diellit Pellazgjik"(Pelasgian traces in Tomor. Symbol of the Pelasgian Sun), Published on the Portal "Dodonanews.Net" on November 5, 2017. With the permission of the researcher Valter

Koxhaj. Or search for this link;
"https://dodonanews.net/gjurme-pellazgjike-ne-tomor-simboli-diellit-pellazgjik-altin-kocaqi/?fbclid=IwAR1LdzVGNOI5oRBm2MVGHzV9pV_ww6DDPjd0)

9- Ceka H. "Notes from the historical geography of Southern Illyria" published in the Magazine "Iliria" Number 1 Tirana 1984 (From page 15 to page 26) or see; https://www.persee.fr/doc/iliri_1727-2548_1984_num_14_1_1306?q=Hasan+Ceka+Barguli

10- Hölder A. Schriften der Balkankommission, Antiquarische Abteilung", Published: Wien: 1900 pages 193

11François Charles Hugues Laurent Pouqueville. Travels in Epirus, Albania, Macedonia, and Thessaly, Printed for Sir Richard Phillips and Co, London 1820 Page 18, 20, 21, 22, 23, 28, 51, 53, 57, 88

12- Wlliam Martin Leak ("Travels in Northern Greece", Volume 1, London 1835. Publisher London : Rodwell Page 351 and 380 and Travels in northern Greece / Vol. 3, Publisher London : Rodwell, page 328.

13- Lear E., Journals of a landscape painter in Albania, & c
Publisher London R. Bentley (1851) page 176, 178.

14- Kristoforidhi K. Gjahu i Malesoreve(Hieja e Tomorrit), Publisher; Nderrmarrja Shteterore e

Botimeve dhe Shperndarjes, Tirana 1950 Pp 17, 18, 19.

15- Vreto J., Vepra te Zgjedhura (Apologjia) Publisher Shtëpia Botuese Naim Frashëri, Tirana 1973 P. 84

17. Sokoli R., Gjeneza e Flamurit dhe Himni Kombëtar. P. 2
https://pdfslide.net/documents/02-ramadan-sokoli-gjeneza-02.html?page=1

18- Vaso P., Translated by; Maci S., E vërteta mbi Shqipërinë dhe shqiptarët (një studim kritik historik). Publisher Argeta-LMG, 2010. Pp. 12, 13.

19- Elsie R., A Reader of Historical Texts, 11th-17th Centuries, Publisher 2003 Harrassowitz Verlag Wiesbaden p.51

20- Galanti A., L'Albania; notizie geografiche, ethnografiche e storiche, Arturo, Rome 1901, Societa Editice Dante Alighieri. P. 30

21- Hopf C., Chroniques gréco-romanes inédites ou peu connues. Berlin Librairie De Weidmann 1873, p. 296.

22- Ermal H. Bazes, Te dhena Arkeologjike per prehistorin ne Qarkun e Beratit. Tirane. Pp. 74.

23- Sir Evans A., Anitquarian Researches in Illyricum, Parts I and II. Printed by Nichols and Sons, 25, Parliament Street. 1883. P.38

24 - Imhoof-Blumer, F., Monnaies grecques. Publisher Amsterdam : Johannes Muller. 1883, See the photos of the coins at the end of the book

25- John Maunsell Frampton May, The Coinage of Damastion and the Lesser Coinages of the Illyro-Paeonian Region", Publisher Scientia Verlag. 1979, p.3

26- Co-authors I. E. S. Edwards, C. J. Gadd, N. G. L. Hammond, E. Sollberger. History Volume II Part 1: History of the Middle East and the Aegean Region c. 1800-1380 B. C. (Third Edition), page 266.

27- John Anthony Cramer. A Geographical and Historical Description of Ancient Greece: Volume 1. Publisher Oxford At The Clarendon Press. Pp. 127

28- Lurker M. A Dictionary of Gods and Goddesses, Devils and Demons. Translated from the German by G. L. Campbell. This translation published Routledge Kegan Paul 1987. Pp.350

29- Elsie R. Balkanistica13 (2000), pp. 35-57 or His article "The Christian Saints of Albania". https://albanianhistory.org/elsie-de/pdf/articles/A2000ChristianSaints.pdf,

30- Tagliavini C. History of pagan and Christian words
through the times. Published by Morcelliana Italy, 1963. Pp. 103

31- Finlay G., Editor:H. F. Tozer, A History of Greece From Its Conquest by the Romans to the Present Time, B.C. 146 to A.D. 1864 · Volume 2

Publisher: Cambridge University Press· 2014. P.381

32- Mane Sh., "Rrethi i Beratit", Iliria Magazine, Year 1976 volume 6 page 405-406 or see; https://www.persee.fr/doc/iliri_1727-2548_1976_num_6_1_1930

33- Theopompo Celebratur, Pliny, book. VI, 7 and VIII, 8, 17

34- Stratton F. H. DODONA. MCMXXXVII PRIVATELY PRINTED PHILADELPHIA, USA 1937. Page 68-88. 74

35- Ν. Β. ΠΑΤΣΕΛΗ. ΟΙ ΠΟΛΙΤΙΚΟΙ ΑΝΔΡΕΣ ΤΗΣ ΗΠΕΙΡΟ. Published ΑΝΑΤΥΠΟΝ ΕΚ ΤΩΝ ΣΤ' ΚΑΙ Ζ ΤΟΜΩΝ ΤΗΣ ΗΠΕΙΡΩΤΙΚΗΣ ΕΣΤΙΑΣ ΙΩΑΝΝΙΝΑ 1955. Pg. 4-10.
(Patcilis B. N.. "Men of the State of Epirus" by Nicolaus, Ioannina 1959, page 4 -10)

36- Iliad- Homer. II, 748-750. 750 BC

37 - Kocaqi A. Dervishi B. "Albanians Pray in the Shadow of Tomor and Have Albanian for the Sign of God", published on June 20, 2015 on the portal "Iliriatv.com.

38- Plutarch "The Parallel Lives" (1. V, 19 1. VI, 21, VIII, 4 and IX, 6) quoted by Perikli Ikonomi on pages 9 and 10 of his book "History of Tomor. Pelasgian Dodona And Tomor God of the Pelasgians".

39- Strabo: Geography VII (7.7) - VIII.
Quote from Peikli Ikonomi in his book; "History of Tomor.Pelasgian Dodona and Tomor God of the Pelasgians " in page 11. Or see;

40- Illyrians and Ancient Authors" with co-authors Frano Prendi, Hasan Ceka, Selim Islami and Skender Anamali as well as translators of Greek-Latin texts Sotir Papakristo, Stefan Prifti, Pashko Geci Henrik Lacaj, Kole Shiroka and Koco Bozhori. Year of publication Prishtina, Kosovo 1979, printing house "Rilindja" p. 161

41-Titus Livy's book "The History of Rome: The Twentieth to the Thirtieth Books, Volume 2" page 159

42- Livy T. book XXIX 12

43- Ceka. N. La Viile Illyrienne de la Basse - Selce, Iliria II 1972, p. 97/8

44- Homer, Iliada I 3. 837; Iliad xx . 223, Iliad XXII lines 30 and 38
750 BC.

45- Gatti E. GLI ETRUSCHI (Rome 1979) Publisher Frama Sud, page 23, 25, 44, 48, 134, 153

46- Aeschylus Book VII, 8 and VIII, 3 quote Ikonomi P.

47- Skymnos Hios (Geography 1, III, 22, VI, 6 VII, 6) quotes Ikonomi P. (page 11)

48- Hall P. M., The Secret Teachings of All Ages. Originally published; Los Angeles, Calif.: Philosophical Research Society, 1928. Reader's Edition first Published by Jeremy P. Tarcher Penguin 2003. Pp. 62, 85, 86, 176, 177, 182, 183, 187, 208, 209, 278

49- Tomorri A. , Historija e Bektashinjeve[Tirane 1929] pp 82-94 Translated from Albanian by Robert Elsie. And Excerpt from Robert Elsie, The Albanian Bektashi History and Culture of a Dervish Order in the Balkan [Great Britain 2019 p. 81

50- General Salle. In this article with the title "The Customs and Legends of Albania" from Revue Bleue, December 3, year 1922, published in the book "The Living Age", Eight Series, Volume XXVI, Boston "The Living Age Company" year 1922, p.44, p.45.

51- Show: "Histori shqiptare", Alma Cupi - Shtegu i panjohur i malit te Tomorrit! (17 shkurt 2018). Minutes from 18:40 - 19:00, TV KLAN. Or you can watch in this link
https://www.youtube.com/watch?v=SlY1xVnBBmM&t=1157s

52- Arthur Bernard Cook, "Zeus A Study in Ancient Religion · Volume 3, Part 2" page 63 and 70. Londer 1940.

53- "The Power of Place: Sacred Sites and the Presence of the Miraculous, Martin Gray, June 17, 202.
Web: https://www.youtube.com/watch?v=IMHTlOJ

103

rzX0&t=66s

54- Kreisberg G. " Did Ancient Humans Have Knowledge of the Electromagnetic (EM) Spectrum?" Author links:overlookmountain.org
Published 21st November 2005 or see; https://grahamhancock.com/kreisberggl

55- Pliny : Natural History iv . 35 and viu . 67

56- Graves R. The Greek Myths, Published New York,G. Braziller,1957, Volume One, Chapter "THE PELASGIAN CREATION MYTH", page 27-28

57- Zotaj M. "The Oracle of Dodona". Published for the first time by Altin Bogdani in the link https://altibogdani.blogspot.com/2012/04/orakulli-i-dodonesnga-frimason-maksim.html?fbclid=IwAR0tqQfi2mQidHAdsC_t4Y9Zn0kPfQ001FX_cp-Z9PFe4TP-8Hgz6CTMhlk

58- Tirta M. Mythology among Albanians",, publication of the Academy of Sciences of Albania, 2004, page 36, 62, 66, 119, 153

59- Spahiu H. Article ; Ekspeditë përnjohëse në rrethet e Beratit dhe të Skraparit, Iliria Magazine, vol. VII- VIII, page 347-348 or see; https://www.persee.fr/doc/iliri_1727-2548_1977_num_7_1_1300

60- Ceka N. Article; Vështrim mbi zhvillimin e jetës qytetare tek Ilirët e Jugut (OVERVIEW OF THE DEVELOPMENT OF CIVIL LIFE IN THE SOUTH ILLIRIS) ILIRIA MAGAZINE 2, 1985 page 132 or see;

https://www.persee.fr/doc/iliri_1727-2548_1985_num_15_2_1361

61- Vlora E. Aus Berat und vom Tomor Published: Sarajevo, D.A. Kajon, 1911. Pp 99- 196, 166-167. 190
"From Berat to Tomor and returns", Author "Eqerem Bej Vlora" pages 166-167, published in Sarajevo, Bosnia and Herzegovina in 1911 in German, translated and republished by the printing house "Koci" in Tirana in 2001. Pp 170-171

62 Book "Folklore" Volume I, 1939 pages 37-38. Or Traces of a primitive calendar in our people ", Rrok Zojzi, year 1949

63 On the Bektashi order and its syncretism of Islam with Christianity see G. Jacob Die Bektaschijjc (Abh. d. layer. Akad. Philosphilol. Classe xxiv. 3. 2) Munich 1909 pp. 1—53 figs. 1—3, a.

64- F. W. Hasluck Christianity and Islam under the Sultans Oxford 1929)
(Bektashi tekke on, 1633, 548: Abbas AH haunts, 932, 548, 548s: gold plant on, 645)

65- Ininerari Albanesi, Antonio Baldacci, 1892, published "La Societa Geografica Italiana p. 87

66- See; (Hesych. Tmarion in Arkadia), (H. Krahe Die alten balkan-illyrischen geographischen Namen Heidelberg 1925 p. 58), (N. Jokl in Ebert Reallex.vi. 34 decides for the latter).

E. Polaschek in Pauly—Wissowa Real-Enc. vi A. 1697 f

N. Jokl in Ebert Reallex.vi. 34 decides for the latter. Quote, the British historian A. B. Cook Zeus: a study in ancient religion (Band 3,2): Zeus god of the dark sky (earthquake, clouds, wind, dew, rain, meteorits): — Cambridge, 1940

67- "The Photo Collection of Erich von Luckwald"- Albania in 1936 — 1941" (Albanien: Land zwischen Gestern und Morgen (Albania: Country between Yesterday and Tomorrow), Munich 1942), published on his website "Robert Elsie Early Photography in Albania"
Or
see; http://www.albanianphotography.net/luckwald/

68- Setton M. K. "The Papacy and the Levant 1204- 1571, Volume II, page 194, USA 1978.

69- Kocaqi A. "Vendi i Shqipes Nder Gjuhet Evropiane" Tirane 2013, page 142

70- Muci S. Bylis page 173, Tirana 1987

71- Stephen C. Duer, Allan B. Smith, " Cypress Hills Cemetery" Publisher:Arcadia Pub. 2010, Page 116

72- B. Bushell W. S. Chinese Art: - Volume 1 - Page 139, 1904

73- Kurilo A. The Symbols of the Constructor: Symbolic Architecture", published in 2014 PG 81-

74- A Geographical and Historical Description of Ancient Greece: With ..., Volume 1", John Anthony Cramer, page127

75- Plutarch (I, V, 19. I, VI, 21, 7, IV.IX, 6) quotes by Perikli Ikonomi In his book "The Pelasgian Dodona and Tomor the God of the Pelasgians" pages 9 and 10.

76- Lurker M. A Dictionary of Gods and Goddesses, Devils and Demons" - London 1988.

77 Ptolemy, Claudius Ptolemy - Theatrum Geographiae Veteris by AncientHistoryMaps. Publication date 1618. Page 32.

78-Storia di parole pagane e christiane attraverso i tempi" (History of pagan and Christian words through the times), published in 1963 by Morcelliana Italy, on page 103

79-The Routledge Dictionary of Gods and Goddesses, Devils and Demons, Manfred Lurker, pg. 55, 57, first published 3rd edition, This Edition published in the Taylor&Francis e- Library 2005. First Published in German in 1984

80- Civilization past and present" by Wallbank, T. Walter (Thomas Walter), 1901, pg.29

81- Hesiod (book Theogony 212-229-232)

82- "GREEK AND ROMAN MYTHOLOGY", by Jessie

M. Tatlock, New York The Century Co. 1921, page 7

83- Helmet of the National Hero of Albania George Kastrioti Skanderbeg. published on the official website of the National Historical Museum in Tirana, Albania in January,8, 2018, on the social network Facebook, with the note.

84- History of Rome" XXIX 12, Titus Liv. Or the book The History of Rome, Volume 4 "Author TITUS LIVIUS (59 B.C- A.D. 17) FQ.214..LONDON 1921.

85- N. Pajakowski, «Starozytny Epir i jego mieszkancy» Poznan 1970, p. 92.
S. Islami (Illyrian State in the War Against Rome, Iliria Magazine number III, 1974 p. 23, note 97
Archaeologist Neritan Ceka (La Viile Illyrienne de la Basse - Selce, Iliria II 1972, p. 97/8.
Quote from Ceka Hasan On page 21 of his study entitled "Notes from the historical geography of Southern Illyria" published in the Magazine "Iliria" Number 1 Tirana 1984 (From page 15 to page 26) or see;
https://www.persee.fr/doc/iliri_1727-2548_1984_num_14_1_1306

86- Breve the memory of the dissident of our house Musachi. Per Giovanni Musachi, despot of Epirus (1555). Published in: Greco-Roman chronicles of Indians or their peacocks published with genealogical notes and tables, ed. Charles Hopf, Berlin, 1873, p. 270 340. Translated from the Italian by Robert Elsie. First published in R. Elsie: Early Albania, a Reader of Historical Texts, 11th - 17th Centuries, Wiesbaden 2003, p. 34-55.

87- Quoted by Maksim Zotaj "The Oracle of Dodona" who had quoted Enzo Gatti, "Gli Iliri" Albanian Publications "Illyrians", pages.87-88,93-94, publisher "Bargjini and with the translation of Rudina Taraneshi and Amik Kasoruho, Tirana, 2005.

88- "Memories" by Ansimo Aleksudhi,
 Corfu Greece, year of publication 1865, page 34

89-"From Tomori of Berat to Tomori of Ioanina", Prof. Ramadan Sokoli, published by Lazer and Jozef Radi
Or see; https://www.radiandradi.com/nga-tomorri-i-beratit-ne-tomorrin-e-janines-prof-ramadan-isuf-sokoli/

90 -Illyrian state in the wars against Rome (231 - 168 BC) Selim Islami, Iliria Magazine year 1974 No. 3 pages. 27, quoted by Titus Livy, History of Rome XXXI 27
Or see https://www.persee.fr/doc/iliri_1727-2548_1974_num_3_1_1151#:~:text=Selim%20ISLAMI%20SHTETI%20ILIR%20N%C3%8B%20LUFTAT%20KUND%C3%8BR,ROM%C3%8BS%20%28231%20%E2%80%94%20168%20para%20e%2C%20son%C3%AB%29

91- F. Prendi - Dh. Budina, Irmaj Castle (excavations of 1960) «BUSHT, social sciences series», 3. Tirana 1964 p. 45 or see https://www.persee.fr/doc/iliri_1727-2548_1972_num_2_1_1141

92- Ylli L. "Random discoveries in Skrapar" published in Iliria Magazine Nr.2 1981 pg. 265 or see;
https://www.persee.fr/doc/iliri_1727-2548_1981_num_11_2_1775?q=zbulime+te+rastit

93- Ylli L. "Archaeological Excavations of 1990" Vlushe Skrapar. Author Luftim Ylli, Iliria Magazine Nr. 2 1990 page 249 or see
https://www.persee.fr/doc/iliri_1727-2548_1990_num_20_2_2023?q=lUFTIM+yLLI+vLUSHE

94- Pilika Dh.. The Pelasgians, our denied origin, who are the descendants of the Pelasgians: monograph. Publisher
Botimet Enciklopedike, Tirane 2005

95 - Hangen, Eva Catherine. Symbols, our universal language. Publisher North Hollywood, Calif. : Symbols & Signs. 1980. Pp. 92

96- Elsie R. (see. Again Balkanistica13 (2000), pp. 35-57 or his article " The Christian Saints of Albania")
https://albanianhistory.org/elsie-de/pdf/articles/A2000ChristianSaints.pdf

97 -Baldacci A. , "Itinerari albanesi (1892)", publisher; La Societa Geografica Italiana, page. 101

98 - "DOCUMENTARY" POLIFONIA LABE
"Published by the former CHANNEL ONE Television

on May 2, 2012: See min. 3:20 - 4:08 .... THE LEGEND OF LABE POLYPHONY. Or click on this link

https://www.youtube.com/watch?v=Vfvu5HOokbI&ab_channel=web4videoch1

99- The Delphic oracle, its early history, influence and fall" the author T. Dempsey on pages 16 -17

100 - Folklore" Volume I, 1939 pages 37-38. Traces of a primitive calendar in our people ", Rrok Zojzi, year 1949,
Or see;
https://www.youtube.com/watch?v=Q6FJgDNK9y8&ab_channel=mallakastrioti

101- A.B. Cook "Zeus: a study in ancient religion (Band 3,2): Zeus god of the dark sky (earthquake, clouds, wind, dew, rain — Cambridge, 1940. But see and On the Bektashi order and its syncretism of Islam with Christianity see G. Jacob Die Bektaschijjc (Abh. d. layer. Akad. Philosphilol. Classe xxiv. 3. 2) Munich 1909 pp. 1—53 figs. 1—3, a.
Also F. W. Hasluck Christianity and Islam under the Sultans Oxford 1929)
(Bektashi tekke on, 1633, 548: Abbas AH haunts, 932, 548, 548s: gold plant on, 645

DEDICATION

Finally, I want to greet my family who supported me in this endeavor, my father, Njazi Dervishi; my mother, Mystafere Dervishi; my brother and sister, Zamir Dervishi and Artiana Dervishi and of course, my wife, Klodiana (Qama) Dervishi. This book is a small contribution that tomorrow will take the place it deserves in my children's library - Albion, Aaron, and Aida. I also want to remember my grandparents, who influenced me with their stories, Rasim and Ferruze Dervishi, Demir and Razije Ibro (Tataja).

I also want to greet the residents of the area of Tomori in Albania who have helped me with valuable information such as;
Nori Pelivani, Adriatik Salillari, Berti Salillari, Krenar Kajo, Rajmonda (Bajraktari) Bala, Fatbardh Bajraktari, Sofokli Mjeshtri, Kristofor Mjeshtri, Liri Dhaskali, Gjergj Zogaj, historian Valter Koxhaj, Artur Guni, Kadri Talaj, Tomorr Laze, Gazmend Shehu, Medi Canko, Zaim Gode, Besnik Gojka, Archaeologist and researcher from Poland Tomasz Lelewski, Argid Kaci, Archaeologist Etnor Canaj, Nexh Goduni, Xelal Licollari, Gjergji Qafoku, Robert Qama, Njazi Dervishi, Fjorentin Allajbeu, Cimi Kora, Gezim Hysi, Regina Sina, Klodian Ibro, Memi Cela, Behar Cela, Engjell Qato, archaeologist Eugen Kallfani, Fadil Kapllani, Demir Ago, Aleksander Muca, Adriana Topore, Elsion Ruka, Albert Laze, Gezim Tare, Ardit Bajraktari, Granit Koroni, A. Boduri, Xhemajl Gashi, Muharrem Abazaj, Fatjon Kora, T. Xhaferraj., Eljo Shenaj, Erind Maliqaj, others
Thank you, and happy reading!

www.ingramcontent.com/pod-product-compliance
Lightning Source LLC
Chambersburg PA
CBHW070906160426
43194CB00034B/2407